Enjoy every moment, they are all filled with blessings, With Love Calynda

Journals of A Loved One

A Memoir & Mission

Calynda Triffo

Life & Executive Coach

Self-Published

Calynda Triffo Holistic Coaching & Therapy

www.calyndatriffo.com

Cover design by Calynda Triffo
Book design by Calynda Triffo
Edited by Jeanne Triffo & Portia Nichol

ISBN: 978-0-995335301

FOREWORD

This book is inspired by the life of Allen Triffo with the mission of raising awareness of how important it is to have a diagnosis as quickly as possible when illness strikes.

Meetings have taken place to discuss options of getting additional diagnostic equipment in Regina, Saskatchewan. The intention is for patients facing critical illness to get a diagnosis quickly rather than spending weeks or months suffering with debilitating worry.

Treatment does not start without a diagnosis. How can a cure be found without knowing the cause?

It is clear that there is a passion and common interest to ease the stress for patients and families faced with illness. A confirmed diagnosis can help with the journey to acceptance and treatment options are more likely with early detection.

Working together as a community, I am confident it is possible to get the diagnostic equipment required to offer patients the ability to get diagnosis in a day rather than having to wait weeks or months.

Visit www.calyndatriffo.com to get updates on progress.

THANK YOU

Sandra, Corie, Taya, Tiana | Trained by the best, it is a blessing to be a part of team Triffo. You are the ones that understand, without words required, because you have already lived, learned and survived this experience with me. There are no words to describe our loss, but it is a relief to know that when crisis strikes, we are able to handle anything together and somehow manage to come out of the situation stronger. Thank you for your unconditional support.

Portia, Jeanne, Randy, Linda, Gordon, Leonard, Edna, Rob & Charlotte | We would not have made it through this journey without you. Thank you for your love and support during this most trying time. You helped make the journey lighter with your contributions: helping with the move, going for lunches, sitting with Dad to give us a break, bringing things to the hospital, helping with the book and just being there when we needed you the most. We are forever grateful for everything you have done and continue to do.

To our friends, family and co-workers | Thank you for your understanding while we faced the worst nightmare imaginable. We appreciated the visits and help accommodating his food requests, with short notice. The memories you shared with him helped with passing the tough moments.

Nurses on 4A at the Pasqua Hospital | Thank you for all of your hard work and dedication. The time Dad spent on the unit was challenging, but he appreciated everything you did for him. He came back to visit to let some of the nurses know that he planned to get better so he could talk to whoever he needed to for changes to be made. Cancer prevented him from doing that. May his story help make improvements for doctors, nurses, hospital staff and future patients.

Dr. Ferguson | We never forgot the conversation our family had with you when the options for available treatment plans were being presented. It was a difficult day for our family, as Dad was faced with making a decision that no one would ever want to make. As a loved one, it was unbearable knowing that there was nothing that could be done to beat the cancer. The only thing we could do was be sure that he understood the options and provide unconditional support with whatever he chose to do. That day, you said a PET scanner would be a big help in helping your patients. The mission is to have necessary diagnostic equipment available to make it easier for all doctors and patients to get an accurate diagnosis quickly. Our hope is that it will help detect critical illness soon enough to allow time for patients to have a chance for more options, including survival. May these efforts help to reduce the number of times you have to inform your patients that the odds are not in their favour.

Thank you for always being gentle with your words and listening to Dad. You provided him with peace. He knew that you did everything within your power to help him and respected your advice. He was grateful for you.

Dr. Dolota | Thank you for always making the bad news bearable, sharing your stories, being honest with your opinions for treatment, doing whatever was necessary to bring Dad peace and always honoring his choices. You gave Dad the chance to appreciate his good minutes and always went above and beyond to help him.

Our family sincerely appreciates that you took the time to send a sympathy card from you and your team.

3B Nurses | There were so many amazing nurses in the several months that he spent on this ward. A few of them saw right through Dad's rough edges to his golden heart.

On 3B, there was a nurse that was amazing with getting the IV's into his tricky rolling veins and he would always joke with her. He let her know of his plan to make her a "Best Nurse Ever" plaque if he started to feel better. When he realized that he wasn't getting his strength back, he decided to donate two framed pictures to this ward of the hospital instead. The pictures were of the first farm house he lived in. When discussing what he wanted to be engraved on the plate, he decided he wanted it donated to all of the nurses, not just one in particular, because he thought the other nurses would feel unappreciated. That wouldn't be fair because they all did the best they could, always. The pictures were donated in appreciation of all nurses on the ward. Thank you all for your constant compassion and understanding.

3A Nurses | It takes a special type of person, with a huge heart, to help families transition from fighting to letting go.

The care, effort and demands required from these nurses is unbelievable. They manage everyday with tremendous grace, understanding and peace, while always going above and beyond to accommodate the needs of everyone around them.

You are all truly angels in scrubs!

Thank you. Thank you. Thank you. Thank you.

Journals of A Loved One

A MEMOIR & MISSION

My Dad, Allen Triffo, refused to travel by airplane. He had a fear of heights and could not bear the thought of having his feet off the ground. The thought of leaving his life in the hands of a pilot made him uneasy. When he wanted to go somewhere, he travelled by vehicle and was usually the driver.

He enjoyed being at home and often questioned why anyone wanted to travel outside of Canada because there was so much to see. He refused to get the internet or learn how to use it. If he wanted to know what a place looked like, and couldn't drive there himself, he looked at pictures and that was good enough.

Once in a while he would entertain the notion of flying and would say if he ever did get on a plane, that he would sit in the cockpit as the co-pilot. It is probably best that he kept his feet on the ground. If he could have overcome his fear of flying, I'm confident he would have been fascinated by it.

On June 17th, three days before his funeral, I was booked on a red eye flight to Edmonton and was scheduled to be back in Regina by midnight. That evening, settled in my seat on the airplane, I was gazing out the window remembering Dad's perspective on flying. It was my sixth flight in seven days and I was exhausted.

As the plane took off and started to climb, my thoughts drifted. My mind was consumed with questions about what it is really like when someone passes away.

Does their spirit become a part of those they love continuing to exist through the thoughts and memories of their loved ones? Are they seeing what their loved ones see? Are they reunited with their loved ones that passed on before them?

Does God actually meet them when they die? Do they instantly know all the answers to the questions that we all spend a lifetime trying to figure out? Is their soul everywhere, or are they in limbo until a judgement day? Are they aware that they passed away? Do they just take their last breath and then that is it, life just stops?

With so many ideas, opinions, religions and scientific believes, who is actually right? No one truly knows. There have been wars and debates for centuries over such topics and the answers still come down to individual beliefs and opinions. For support, people join organizations, associations and groups with similar understanding or belief systems. It is all based on faith or theory. Ideas based on perspective. When perspective shifts, ideas change.

Theory is proven by extensive observation, experimentation and testing, but as new developments arise, theories change. This leads to a new hypothesis and the cycle continues.

How does one prove faith? We can't see it or touch it. The options are believe or do not believe.

To my knowledge, there is no one that can actually answer any of those questions with solid evidence. It comes down to who can debate better.

These questions continued to consume my thoughts as the plane made its way over the clouds. My heart yearned for peace. It wasn't long before the questions were replaced with the thought, "Dad, I just wish there was some way that you could tell me that you are okay".

I desperately hoped that he was at peace. Enjoying time reunited with his family, in the beautiful space that people refer to as heaven. Looking out the window at the checkered fields getting smaller, the plane climbed higher and passed through the clouds.

I started to cry for the first time since he passed away eighteen days prior. Thank goodness no one was sitting beside me as the tears streamed down my face and my heart shattered all over again. In that moment, knowing his suffering was over was more important than any of the other questions.

Continuing to look out the window, a heart-shaped rainbow appeared above the clouds. Thinking that it was somehow caused from my crying, I wiped away my tears, but the image was still there.

My next thought was that I was overtired and starting to hallucinate. In 42 years, I had never seen a rainbow in that shape and was in shock. Blinking to be sure it wasn't my eyes playing tricks on me, I stared at it for what felt like forever. Flying as fast as planes fly, the heart-shaped rainbow wasn't going away.

I started scrambling for my purse to get my iPad. My thought process was if the camera lens captured the image, it had to be real. Of course I had turned off the device before take-off, so I had to wait for it to power back on. Then made sure it was in airplane mode so it wouldn't do whatever cellular signals do to planes when they are turned on. Finally, I opened the camera app and took the picture.

The heart-shaped image had faded and was changing shape by the time I got organized. I snapped photos anyway as the colours made their way into a perfect circle beyond the wing of the plane. I was able to get several pictures of the circle rainbow over the span of two minutes, including the one that is used for the cover of this book. In the final photo, the rainbow looked to me like it was in the shape of an old style keyhole.

From what I've read, the science behind circle rainbows is controversial, just like everything else. I do not understand how the images could appear for so long outside of a moving plane window but I am grateful for seeing them when I did.

Simply put, just enjoy the good minutes. Isn't that how a journey with a loved one should be? For me, it was summed up in two minutes with a rainbow that had the ability to change shape. Having the opportunity to enjoy the view before it disappeared, making the best of the experience, capturing the moment and just be present are great lessons for anyone to learn.

I had been on 23 flights in six months. I was, and still am, guilty of looking for that circle rainbow every time that I am on an airplane.

Our family had been under tremendous stress for over a year and were all working too much. A break and some excitement were long overdue. We all knew we needed to get away, and had talked about a few locations, but Las Vegas was the popular choice.

Corie, my brother, made the final decision that the family was going to Las Vegas while the rest of us contemplated and made up excuses. Leaving became non-negotiable when he booked the trip and bought the tickets. It was official, my Mom, Sandra, was scheduled to take the first flight of her life on Christmas Eve, at age 63. Generally nervous about the thought of flying, she was fine in the days leading up to our departure.

Mom was excited as she boarded the plane on December 24, 2015 with Taya and Tiana, her granddaughters, and I, to join Corie in Las Vegas for the holidays. It was on that flight we saw the circle rainbow again. Tiana, my youngest daughter, was able to take a picture of it on her iPod. Like the first one, it lasted about two minutes before fading. It is still a mystery to me how a circle rainbow can appear for that long with a plane flying as fast as it does, with impeccable timing. My questions remain unanswered.

After seeing the rainbows, there is no way to prove if what I believe is right or wrong. I'm left to my ideas of what it could be and I will leave you to yours.

Allen fought for every moment he got and we were blessed to have him for as long as we did. The best we can do to honor his memory is to live every moment to the fullest. That's what he would want. He spent every day of his life focused on accomplishing something and usually succeeded.

He will be forever loved by his wife, children, grandchildren, family and friends.

~ Calynda Triffo

ABOUT ALLEN

The Early Years

On June 20, 1948, Allen Triffo, a strong willed boy, was born the eighth child of Mary and Louis in Strasbourg, Saskatchewan.

The earliest memory he had was throwing his glass baby bottles over the edge of his crib to watch them break as they hit the floor. One day he threw his bottle and, to his dismay, he never got another one.

Allen's first years were spent at their home on the farm. It was a stone house by Fox's Point before the family moved to a tiny farm house by Last Mountain Lake.

In 1954, when Allen was only five years old, his Dad got very sick and had to go to the hospital. He remembered the day his Dad left the farm. It was the last time he saw him. The family got the news that Louis passed away at the age of 44. It was a memory that affected Allen for the rest of his life. He thought about his Dad often and always missed him.

Mary was a widow with nine children and little means to provide for them. The family moved from the farm to a small house at 214 Gastle Street in Strasbourg, Saskatchewan. This is where Allen spent the remainder of his childhood growing up.

He attended grade school at Strasbourg School. There were two kids named Allan in his class. For the teacher to keep the boys' school work straight, she had him spell his name Allen instead of Allan.

It stuck and that's how he always spelled it. This caused some confusion when his family realized that how his name was spelled on his identification was different than what they were accustomed to spelling it and they continue to be inconsistent when writing his name.

His Mom, who was referred to as Granny by everyone after her first grandchild was born, was an amazing and strong woman with patience and a heart of gold. Her hard work, strength, love, sense of humor and cooking were always appreciated.

Allen was her youngest son. She called him her "Little Ally".

He took up supervising when he was very young. Mary was an incredible cook, but Allen was convinced that his Mom required his guidance in the kitchen. She let him help, taught him everything he knew and he was always happy to spend time with her.

When he left home, the kitchen supervision continued with everyone else, except for maybe his mother-in-law. The best a cook could hope for would be to have Allen keep a watchful eye over their shoulder while giving play-by-play instructions on what to do next.

If procedures were not being followed the way he thought they should be, the cook would be evicted from the kitchen and he would take over. It was a rare occasion to prepare anything without him and he usually took the credit for the finished product. If he was making stew, he was left alone to create his masterpiece. That was his signature dish and one of the family favorites.

His talents and supervision did not stop in the kitchen. Fixing things was his specialty. He had a natural talent for working with anything mechanical and building things. While most people hire out a job or search YouTube for help, he just thought logically about things and came up with a solution.

If anyone needed something done, it didn't take him long to get his tools and he would be there to help.

When working on a project, he had a certain way of doing things. The first step was making a plan. Once he thought that through, he would get to work.

There would be times that he would stop production because he would get a different idea or something wasn't working.

He would go back, think things through again, adjust and continue until the project was complete. The finished product was always amazing.

If there was a helper with different ideas, he would listen, think about the suggestion, and calculate what it would be like when it was finished, then decide which way would be best. Usually, he was right. He was smart and talented.

It was a rare occasion that he had to hire anyone to do anything. He preferred do things himself so things would get done right.

He was a hard worker and was happiest when he was doing something productive. He wasn't one to sit around and let time pass by. Even when he was sick and in pain, he kept going.

Allen was a man of his word, a handshake was enough. If he said it, he did it. He wasn't one to express his emotions with words, but instead relied on his actions to show how he felt.

Allen had a sense of humor that is hard to describe. He could be a pest and drive a person crazy when he started poking fun.

If someone else was in the room watching, he would look at them with a crooked smile and wink, letting them know that he was just joking and was having fun at someone else's expense.

He would make the weirdest faces, say the funniest things and had the goofiest moves. You couldn't help but laugh at him and he enjoyed that.

There was never a dull moment with him around.

Married

In his early twenties, Allen was introduced to the love of his life. He met Sandra, through family connections.

They dated for a couple of years before getting married on October 5, 1974.

From the time they met, they spent most of their time together for over forty years.

Their wedding song was, "Kiss An Angel Good Morning" by Charlie Pride. They were able to listen to it live at concerts several times over the years.

For their honeymoon, they went to Thief River Falls, Minnesota, USA. While they were there, they went to visit Sandra's Dad's family homestead.

Allen gained a mother-in-law, Rosemary, and father-in-law, Roy. They lived on a farm in Midale, Saskatchewan with their two sons.

Allen was welcomed into the family, and enjoyed helping on the farm and spending time with Roy and his brothers-in-law, Gordon and Randy. He liked driving the machinery and working in the fields. There was always something to do.

Roy looked after the dam in Midale and Allen enjoyed going with him to check the water levels.

Rosemary was used to cooking a lot. Every morning, when Allen and Sandra were visiting, they would wake up to the smell of coffee and food cooking. Rose would always be up early making a breakfast that included oatmeal, eggs, bacon and toast. No one ever left the family table hungry.

His father-in-law owned a 1956 Pontiac. Allen really liked that vehicle and always wanted to restore it.

Allen and Sandra enjoyed going to concerts like the Elvis impersonators, Conway Twitty, Mel Tillis, Johnny Cash, Don Williams and Stomping Tom.

A Father

Allen and Sandra had their first child in 1972, a daughter they named Calynda. In 1977, they were blessed with a healthy baby boy, Corie. They had their family and were content having a girl and a boy.

His role as a husband and father were his top priority. He enjoyed taking the family to a zoo, fireworks, parades and the Moose Jaw airshow when the kids were young.

Building forts, skating rinks, igloos, snowmen, tobogganing, making tracks in the snow were some of the fun winter activities that he participated in with his children.

He taught Calynda and Corie how to ride their bikes. He built them swing sets and sandboxes. He would take the family camping and was happy to share his fascination with nature. He also liked to point out historical details of every place they went.

Allen helped his children with school projects, taught them how things worked, drove them to their activities and was there for the school events. He spent time playing board games, cards, building models, putting together puzzles, telling stories and playing video games. Allen was fun to spend time with and could always be counted on by his family.

Allen taught his children to be independent, responsible and resourceful. His family was always his number one priority.

His love for children was obvious and it took little effort for him to earn every letter in the sayings, "World's Greatest Dad" and "World's Greatest Grandpa". It came to him naturally and was just who he was.

His Career

On August 1, 1974, Allen started working at Ipsco in the spiral mill.

Throughout the years, there were several layoffs. There were times that he would get called back to work, and then get notice that he was laid off, in the same day. He would keep these notices. Eventually, he started to roll them together to see how big the roll would get. It was like a pipe of paper by the time he got his last notice.

Most of his closest friendships were with the people that he worked with over the decades at Ipsco. Some of the memories he shared about work were priceless and I'm sure they still bring a smile to the faces of those that remember them. If he had an opinion about something, he was not scared to share it.

In 1999, he received a gold watch for twenty-five years of service. He retired on August 1, 2004 as a mill operator after 30 years of working for the company.

A Grandpa

In November 1997, Allen became a grandpa for the first time. He fell in love with his granddaughter, Taya, at first sight. He often said that if he knew grandchildren were so great he would have had them first.

He was excited to take Taya home from the hospital. He put her in the car seat and buckled it into the van. The first stop was to visit his brother, Art.

When Calynda went to take Taya out of the vehicle, she realized that Allen had buckled the car seat into the vehicle upside down. The baby's head was where her feet should have been but she hadn't fussed about it for the short time she had been in there.

In 1999, Allen was blessed with his second granddaughter, Tiana. His excitement and love were evident the moment he met her. They instantly became best friends and were virtually inseparable.

Allen was very proud of both his granddaughters and often told them that they could move to his house, but he settled for spending time babysitting and visiting them several times in a week.

There wasn't a school activity or sporting event that he missed, unless it was impossible for him to attend.

He always took the time to teach them life skills, spent hours doing arts and crafts with them, taught them how to build and fix things, took them on holidays, camping, adventures around town and would drive them anywhere they needed or wanted to go.

Hospital Adventures

For The Love of Buttermilk

Allen loved buttermilk. His brother Arthur was given some homemade buttermilk, but it had gone bad. The two brothers, with their "waste not, want not" mentality, drank the tainted liquid anyway. A few hours later, Art had a fever and was incredibly ill with stomach cramps. Allen was feeling the same way. The two of them were taken to the emergency for food poisoning, lying side by side in the hallway, entertaining the hospital staff, they tried to justify their reasons for drinking the milk. Ultimately, they came to the conclusion that it would have been a better idea to throw it out.

Kidney Stones

Allen had several kidney stone attacks. One of the worst ones was in 1997 when Calynda was seven months pregnant with his first grandchild. He was taken to emergency in the "worst pain of his life".

During the process of having one of the exams, he was having a conversation with a female technician about how painful kidney stones were while Sandra and Calynda were in the family area waiting for his tests to be completed. The technician had experienced both kidney stones and childbirth and had let him know that kidney stones were more painful. When he came out of the room, he was quick to inform his wife and daughter that he had experienced the worst possible pain. It had been far more painful than labour or childbirth. It was easy to believe that could be true, because he had been in so much agony for so long and looked worn out. Thankfully, he was able to get the kidney stones removed and began to feel better.

Heart Surgery

In 2005, Allen went to the General Hospital in Regina for a stress test. It didn't go well and they wouldn't let him leave. He was admitted to the hospital and was told that the test results showed he was at high risk for a heart attack. Surgery was required. He was put on blood thinner and was informed about the procedure in the days leading up to the surgery.

Initially, it was thought that he would need a triple bypass. The heart surgeons in Regina are incredible. Dr. Moustapha was his surgeon. When they opened him up, there were some complications. It was realized that a triple bypass wouldn't work for the long term and Dr. Moustapha was able to change the procedure to the six heart bypass instead. It was a very long surgery, but Allen came through.

When we got to see him, he was as white as a sheet of paper. He didn't look good, but then his eyes opened. Seeing his brown eyes was an amazing moment and a big relief.

It took about three months for him to get back to normal. When he healed, the scar from his surgery was barely visible when he had his shirt off. He felt amazing and had stopped smoking for four months. Despite his continued smoking against the doctors' advice and needing multiple medications for his ailments, his heart was repaired better than anyone could have hoped for.

With what his heart withstood for the remainder of his life, it proves that Dr. Moustapha's work was above and beyond what could have been expected. Regina is blessed to have such a gifted cardiothoracic team of surgeons at the General Hospital.

Through The Years

1976

Allen, Sandra and his brother, Art, went on a vacation to Ontario. They enjoyed the sites in Dryden, Thunder Bay, Kenora, Red Rock, Sault Ste. Marie, Trout Lake and the Big Nickel Mine in Sudbury.

When they made it to Agawa Canyon, Art and Allen sat under a sign with a bear painted on it. They were disappointed that it was the only wildlife they had the opportunity to see on that entire vacation.

They were among the first million people to go up into the CN Tower in Toronto, Ontario and went on the island ferry.

They climbed 386 steps to the top off Brook Monument in Niagra Falls. When they reached the top, they discovered that the only thing that you could see out of was a tiny port hole.

1977

On September 21, 1977, Allen's brother was tragically killed, at the age of 40, in a single vehicle car accident on highway 20, a mile north of Bulyea, Saskatchewan. He was laid to rest at the Bulyea cemetery beside his father, Louis.

1982

Sandra's father hadn't been feeling well and was admitted to the Midale Hospital. Allen and Sandra went to the farm to help and be with the family.

On July 15, it was stormy weather. After midnight when everyone was asleep, lightning hit the farm yard light. All of the electronics in the house turned on and a loud scratchy static sound bellowed throughout the entire house. Everyone sat up in bed with a jolt, with hair standing on end from the electricity in the air. The power surge damaged most of the technology in the house and they needed to be replaced. Anything electrical was unplugged after that during storms.

The following morning, Allen and Sandra were getting ready to leave when the phone rang. It was the hospital. On July 16, 1982, Allen's father-in-law, Roy, passed away at the age of 73 from a massive heart attack. It was a shock.

After Roy's passing, help was needed on the farm and Allen was happy to contribute when he could. He enjoyed loading bales, combining, cultivating and doing what was needed.

1984

It was the first year that Allen and Sandra started going to the Craven Country Jamboree to listen to country music. In the early years they went with friends and family. Most years it ended up being a mud festival due to the rain.
They would take their chairs and listen to the concerts regardless of weather conditions. Some years, Allen got really ambitious and he would get into the 'gopher run'. This meant sitting in line for hours until the gates opened so he could get the lawn chairs to an area closer to the stage.

That winter, there was a lot of snow on the farm with large snow drifts. Allen hollowed out one of the drifts with Calynda and Corie and it served as a fort providing hours of entertainment for the season.

1985

Corie was in cub scouts and there was a project assigned to build a race car out of a block of wood. This assignment became a very serious matter in the Triffo household. It kept them busy for a while. The car had to be a certain weight and there were rules associated with how it could be built. The car was fast, but didn't achieve the results they had hoped for at the competition.

Allen and Corie graduated from building cars out of wood, to spending time together restoring Corie's vehicles for the race track and car shows with many friends. Over the past couple decades, there have been countless hours, days, months, coffee, cigarettes, debates, car parts, blood, sweat, awards for several cars, of all shapes and sizes, since their humble beginnings with that wood block. Their efforts with these vehicles are all part of many great memories and proud family moments.

1986

Sandra decided that she wanted to have brass door knobs in the house and Allen didn't think that was necessary. When he opened his presents at Christmas he was shocked to see that he got brass door knobs from Santa. He was a good sport and installed them.

1987

The family took a trip to Yellowknife from Regina to visit Allen's brother, sister-in-law and nephew. They had a camper van at the time and left early with the intentions of taking a few days to get there, but it never happened. Allen just kept on driving.

Back then, the last 200 miles on the road to Yellowknife were winding. It was summer time, so the sun only got to the horizon before it started coming back up. It was light despite being after midnight.

Allen had been driving all day and Calynda was sitting in the passenger seat talking to him to keep him awake for this last curvy stretch. Allen would drive around a curve of the winding road and then close his eyes because he was so tired, but he still managed to drive straight. When he approached the next curve, Calynda would yell, "Dad, turn". He would make the turn, then continue to drive straight until the next turn.

Calynda had her learner's licence at the time, but clearly he felt safer driving half asleep at the wheel than having her drive awake on an empty highway.

This process continued until they reached Yellowknife. They arrived safe and it was another adventure with Allen.

That trip they were able to see the Duke and Duchess of York, went for a hike at midnight when it was still daylight and they all received certificates by Canada's Artic North West Territories certifying they crossed the 60th parallel by the Order of Artic Adventures.

1989

A lot of time was spent camping at Rowan's Ravine Provincial Park. Allen would get caught up watching the birds and wildlife, building campfires, setting up camp and telling stories. He always enjoyed being outdoors. The only problem with camping with him was when it was time to go to sleep.

If you've ever watched the episode of the Flintstones where Fred was snoring while camping in a tent, you have the general idea of what it was like camping close to "Big Al". If you have not had the pleasure of watching that episode, he is the reason that people refer to snoring as "sawing logs", it was very loud and relentless.

1991

At the family Christmas party, Allen and his nephew demonstrated a special talent they shared.

Pillows were put on the floor close to the wall. The two men maneuvered themselves into a hand stand position. A mug of beer was placed on the floor in front of them and they had a race to see who could drink the mug of beer, upside down, the fastest.

There is no record of who won, but Allen retired from those competitions after that and passed the torch to his nephew to carry on.

1993

Allen's Mom hadn't been feeling well in the morning. She was in the kitchen and told her long-time friend, Ken, that she was going to lay down. She fell asleep on the couch, but never woke up.

On February 9, 1993, Mary (Granny) Triffo, passed away peacefully at home at the age of 78. She left behind two daughters, a son-in-law, six sons, five daughters-in-law, 19 grandchildren, 12 great grandchildren, three sisters, four brothers, four brothers-in-law, two sisters-in-law, her special friend, Ken, along with several nephews, nieces and friends.

1997

In the spring of 1997, Calynda purchased a condo and Allen spent time helping with minor renovations.

Calynda was pregnant with Allen and Sandra's first grandchild. In November, she was overdue and scheduled to be induced. Allen drove Calynda to the hospital, expecting that she would stay there until the baby was born. That was not the case. She was induced and was being sent home until contractions started. It was no secret that he was not impressed with the hospital policy.

When Calynda was in recovery, she called Allen to let him know that he had a granddaughter and she weighed 9 lbs 1 oz. He was thrilled, but his response was, "Ahh, that's nothing. I have been through worse", referring to his kidney stone attack a few months prior.

When he got to the hospital, he waited for Taya to open her eyes and look at him before he would pick her up. Once she looked at him, he said something to her and then his coat and cigarettes went flying. He just couldn't pick her up quick enough.

It was his first year as a grandpa and Allen was working on Christmas Eve. He received a note from an "Ipsco Elf" that night.

"It was the night before Christmas when everything's still, except for the clatter, from the ol' spiral mill. Production was down, but the foreman can't see, the employee's should be home, with their families.

Then suddenly at nine, we all got a laugh, for here comes a Santa, and the rest of his staff. "The Santa is the head of Spiral," I heard someone say, "I seen him buy that old suit, at the auction today."

All of his elves, were dressed much the same. They had little green jackets, on the front was their name. Their slippers were curled, and their hats, what a sight, but the sweetest of all, was their tight little tights. Each Elf had a bag that was all covered in flies and handed two turtles to each of the guys. They waved Merry Christmas as they went on their way, we stood there dumbfounded with nothing to say. Next Christmas will be different, I promise to you. If I'm scheduled to work, I'll come down with the flu." – Author unknown

1998

On June 20 there was a combined party for Allen's 50th birthday and his brother's retirement. Allen was given a t-shirt that had a picture of Taya on it that read, "My grandpa's 50". He wore it often for over a decade and a half.

1999

In August, Allen was excited and proud to meet his second granddaughter, Tiana.

He would visit his granddaughters several times per week because he never wanted to miss any of their milestones.

Allen was excited to learn of crop circles that appeared in fields just outside of Midale. He travelled to investigate and have pictures taken while standing in the middle of them.

2003

On February 11, Rosemary, Allen's mother-in-law, passed away at 92 in Estevan, Saskatchewan after developing pneumonia.

2004

In January, Allen and Sandra made an attempt at becoming snowbirds. A three month vacation was planned for them to go to Arizona for the winter.

On their way to Arizona, they were hoping for clear roads, but there was snow until they got 60 miles north of Las Vegas, Nevada. For the majority of their holiday, they stayed at the Apache Junction in Mesa Arizona.

While at the campsite, Allen learned how to make airplanes out of pop cans and continued to make several after that for family and friends.

On Valentine's Day, their house in Regina was broken into and several items had been stolen. They stayed on their holiday as scheduled and arrived home on March 17th. It was the end of being snowbirds.

2006

Helping with renovations was one of Allen's favorite hobbies. Corie had purchased his neighbor's house as a rental property. The house had not been updated since it was built. There was a lot of work required because the entire house had to be torn apart to the outside walls for the renovation to be completed properly.

The outside of the house required just as much work as the inside. Corie, Allen and Sandra worked on the house every spare minute they had for three months to get the house restored into a liveable space and they did a great job.

Calynda had recently sold her house and was looking to buy another property. Calynda moved in and purchased the house within the year. Allen continued to find projects to do at Calynda's and enjoyed only needing a ten minute drive to visit his son, daughter and grandchildren all in one location.

2008

Allen was suffering severe back pain due to spondylolisthesis of the spine and required back surgery. The procedure happened a few weeks before his 60th birthday. The family planned a surprise birthday for him with friends and family. They had booked Merv's Pitchfork Fondue to cater the event and had to come up with some creative ideas to find an excuse to get him to leave the house in his condition.

Allen was released from the hospital and could walk a little in time for the party. To get him to the surprise, Corie went to pick him up so he could help him if needed because he was still weak from the back surgery. Allen was under the impression that he was going for family photos.

When they reached Calynda's house, Allen saw the catering trailer and the ninety people that filled the yard to help him celebrate and he went into shock. He spent the day enjoying everyone's company and it lifted his spirits. He started living life to the fullest after that.

Allen and Sandra went to the Craven Country Jamboree with friends that year, and decided to rent a seasonal campsite in Craven World. Allen enjoyed fixing up their camping space to make it a comfortable retreat close to home to spend their summers enjoying the outdoors.

A chair swing, hammock, shed, gazebo, fence and fire pit were quickly set up and they had everything that was needed to relax while enjoying campfire breakfast, coffee, marshmallow roasts, burnt hotdogs and everything else that comes with spending time in nature.

2009

Allen's brother, Arthur had been in an out of hospital since December with what was thought to be pneumonia.

In January, he was undergoing further testing. Later that month he was diagnosed with lung cancer. He would spend the next four months in hospital.

Allen was at the hospital several times per week to visit, would bring his brother whatever he needed and helped him however he could.

In the early hours of April 28, 2009, Allen got a call from Calynda letting him know that the family was being called in. Allen and Sandra went to the hospital shortly after, and joined Allen's niece, to be by his brother's side at 6:28 am, as he passed away peacefully in his sleep.

2010

Corie had decided to build onto his existing garage. Allen was obviously a part of the building committee. There seemed to be a discrepancy on who was actually the project manager.

With Calynda living next door, there was plenty of room for the antique cement mixer to be set up in her back yard to start production for the new garage floor.

In exchange, Calynda had a front row seat to all the entertainment. With windows open in the summer, the two project managers could easily be heard having a debate about how the cement was to be made, one never really listening to the other.

The water, sand and cement mix recipe was the point of contention. One wanted it with less sand so it was thinner and the other insisted that it needed more sand so it was thicker.

The first load of cement was mixed and ready to be poured. It was dumped into the wheel barrel and the recipe according to Corie was put into the cement mixer before he took the wheel barrel to be dumped where it needed to be. The moment that Corie was out of sight, adjustments were made by either adding more sand or more water to the mixer, so the cement would be at the consistency that Allen thought it should be.

Most projects between those two went like this. They never argued, but they never agreed either. It was entertainment at its finest. All that was ever missing was a video camera and a bowl of popcorn, but hindsight is always 20/20.

Allen was helping Corie build the add-on to his garage, but he wasn't feeling well and decided he needed the day off. Tiana decided to help her grandpa by writing a pretend doctors' note for Allen to give to Corie to get the day off from his volunteer position.

The note read:

November 18, 2010

Dr. Truly

Allen is not feeling good so he will not be able to go to work for 2 more days. Please contact me if you find there will not be any time for him to take off.

Signed: *Dr. Truly*   Signed by Patient: *A Triffo*
St. John Clinic

2011

In April, there was a flood in the Qu'Appelle Valley including the campground where Allen and Sandra had their seasonal campsite.

The water took almost a month to go back down before the damages could be assessed.

When the water cleared, Allen and Sandra made the decision to give up their seasonal site, sold the motorhome and officially retired from camping.

2012

A celebration was held for Sandra's 60th birthday. A limo was rented to take the family out for supper and on a tour around town. It was a fun for everyone.

2013

On April 16, Allen lost his brother Len, after a short and courageous battle to pancreatic cancer at the age of 73. Len was recognized as the White Cane Club person of the year and was a volunteer with the Canadian Council of the Blind for nearly 50 years.

In 2010, Len was the recipient of the Award of Merit by the Canadian Council of the Blind. It is the highest honour that the Canadian Council of the Blind can bestow, is a prestigious award, only presented every two years, to a person recommended for outstanding service to the blind, with recommendations having been made by their chapter or division.

On November 24, Allen was excited to attend the 101st Grey Cup in Regina with Corie. They enjoyed watching the game from the box seats as the Saskatchewan Roughriders won the game, at home, against the Hamilton Tiger Cats. It was a very exciting day for Rider Nation.

Allen had been diagnosed with type II diabetes years prior and was on insulin. When his dosage was going to be increased to 80 units, he went onto a paleo diet and worked with his doctor to have his insulin adjusted. His blood sugars improved and he went down to 199 lbs where he stayed for a few years. He wasn't willing to give up the foods he loved, but did start eating them in moderation. He was aware he would need more insulin when he ate certain foods and was content with that.

2014

On February 21, Allen and Sandra had the opportunity to get their picture taken with the Grey Cup.

In the summer, Allen decided to take on the project of putting siding, shingles and repairing the shed at Calynda's. He was passionate about using materials he had to complete projects. It was like he won the lottery every time he found something that could be used for improvements. He worked at his own pace. If anyone tried to help him, he would get frustrated. It was easier on him if he could do it himself.

It was while working on this project that it became apparent Allen wasn't feeling well. He was moving slower than usual, taking lots of breaks, tired easily, was losing weight rapidly, coughing and by August he started to vomit when he ate.

One morning, while he was working on the garage, Calynda noticed he was sitting in his van holding a coffee, like he always did when he took a break, but what he was drinking wasn't staying down. He was getting sick and he started to complain that food was tasting funny. Being a smoker for 56 years, these symptoms had his family concerned and after weeks of trying to convince him, at the beginning of September, he went to visit his family doctor. He was being treated for pneumonia, but often said that he had lung cancer, like his brother Arthur, who passed away in 2009.

Allen was persistent and managed to complete the garage that summer, with as little help as possible.

Allen and Sandra spent many hours enjoying their granddaughters' school events. They were always on the sidelines or in the audience watching basketball, handball, musicals and awards shows. These events were the highlight of the next few months. It gave Allen an opportunity to think of something else than his health.

THE JOURNALS

The Journey Begins

Feeling very ill on September 12, 2014, Dad went to emergency. A mass was detected by his lung and he was sent home that evening.

He had to wait for an appointment to get an MRI, CT scan and bone scan. This brought back all the memories from five years prior, when his brother, Arthur had been diagnosed with lung cancer.

When Corie and I learned of the mass, we both began intensive research in preparation for the worst case scenario. Corie contacted the Mayo Clinic for testing options and spoke with specialists in the USA, while I continued researching alternative health care options. We were desperately searching for anything and everything that had worked for lung cancer because it was what we feared most.

With Dad's long list of health issues and not feeling well, he was not willing to travel by vehicle for long distances. Flying was a non-negotiable for him. The only option was to rely on the Regina Qu'Appelle Healthcare system.

Since the passing of Dad's brother in 2009, I have dedicated most of my spare time to learning how the body works and have studied several holistic modalities. Initially, these journals were being kept to help me understand symptoms and imbalances.

What you are about to read is my diary. It includes stories about the people that are the closest to me, my feelings, thoughts and the challenges we faced, on the toughest journey our family has ever known.

There is a grieving process that occurs when a loved one is diagnosed with a critical illness. It is different with everyone. We supported each other throughout the emotional roller coaster, as a family, while Dad was still with us. Somehow, we managed to gather strength together while our hearts fell apart.

The journals have remained unedited, because the past can't be changed. It is as real as it can be from my perspective on the day that I wrote each journal entry. It will likely differ from how others remember it. When going through the diary to write this book, there were several things I had forgotten and feelings have changed since then.

The decisions to turn the journals into a book was made in the spring of 2015 after Dad experienced his struggles in the health care system. Dad wanted his story told so that he could make a difference, but cancer wasn't going to allow him to do that.

Allowing the public to have access to this information would never be considered if not for a greater purpose. This is a mission as big as this journey is personal. It is to raise the awareness of how important it is to have an accurate diagnosis, as soon as possible. For this to happen, access to diagnostic testing, in a reasonable time frame, is required.

The Allan Blair Clinic only administers to cancer patients. Deciding who takes priority, when diagnostic equipment is overbooked, must be difficult. For some, it is a life and death decision. Illness detected soon enough may provide options. When disease progresses too far, those options may no longer be available.

We met hospital staff that spent long days at the hospital. They put their patients' needs ahead of their own. Some had a loved one of their own facing similar health struggles.

The nurses are assigned to several patients at once. If patients need significant care, nurses are required to run in several directions at the same time. Multi-tasking becomes a necessity and not an option. The nurses touched Dad's heart. He saw first-hand the struggles that they faced and knew that they always did everything they could for him.

Dad approved of me writing a book about his experiences in hopes that his story could encourage improvements within the health care system. He wanted to help others faced with similar situations.

I have my families support with the mission.

May Allen Triffo's memoir help existing and future patients.

These are the journals of a loved one

SHOCK

September 12, 2014

Hearing the news that they found a mass caused immediate panic and tears started to flow. This couldn't be happening to Dad. How was I going to find the strength to watch the pillar of our family, our rock, go through this? He was going to need us to be strong and my girls would need me to lean on.

The grief was overwhelming as I made a deal with myself that I could cry as much as I wanted, but I had to do it within 12 hours to get it out of my system. This time, if he was diagnosed with cancer, I wasn't going to have time to fall apart. That night, I cried myself to sleep and woke up on a drenched pillow.

When someone you love is told they are being tested for cancer, the world as you know it changes. It is just a test with the potential of being cancer, but thoughts filled with fear, concern and worry are hard to avoid. It's terrifying for everyone involved. A minute feels like a day, an hour like a week and a week like a year. Thoughts race and emotions are all over the place. It doesn't take a lot of time to think of every possible outcome. Waiting is the only option.

Wait to see a doctor
Wait to get sent for tests
Wait for the doctor to get the test results
Wait for the next test, wait, wait, wait, wait and wait.

Logically, everyone knows that the mass isn't waiting. It is progressing. Waiting for a diagnosis with the health care system can be emotionally crippling. To help distract Dad while waiting for answers, attempts were made to organize celebrations and focus on having fun.

September 28, 2014

A 40th wedding anniversary party was organized for Mom and Dad with family and friends invited to help them celebrate. I let Dad and Corie in on the secret, but Mom was completely shocked by the event. Without knowing a diagnosis or treatment plan, it was organized as soon as possible prior to their actual anniversary.

Corie was scheduled to be in Las Vegas the day of this celebration, so arrangements were made to have him join by video conference.

Mom and Dad enjoyed having a nice visit with everyone for a few hours. Dad wasn't feeling well, was having problems eating, but managed to gather enough strength to get through the celebration and visit for a while.

October 5, 2014

Allen & Sandra's 40th Wedding Anniversary

The family went to Memories to celebrate.

They got a bottle of champagne that was marked with their anniversary date. It was a lovely evening.

Dad did not feel hungry. He was frustrated because he was having difficulty eating and wasn't enjoying food like he used to. He was tired and weak.

It was quiet, we had a private room, the food was great and service was amazing.

FRUSTRATION

November 2, 2014

It has been over two and a half months since we learned about Dad's mass but we are still waiting for a diagnosis. We need to know what is wrong with him so we can figure out what the next steps will be.

Tonight, Corie was working on a vehicle in his garage with a friend. Dad went over to visit. They were talking when the colour drained from Dad's face and he fainted. Corie's friend called an ambulance and Dad was taken to emergency where they hooked him up to IV.

I was in Ottawa at a conference when I got the call letting me know what had happened. Worry set in and I wanted to go home to be with my family.

While Corie was talking to me on the phone, Dad was commenting in the background that it had happened before. He said he would be better in a while, he just needed time to rest.

This wasn't something he had mentioned to any of us, and hearing that didn't make us feel better. Our concern increased. We need testing done so that we know exactly what is going on.

Dad made it clear that he was annoyed that he had been taken to the hospital because they weren't going to do anything anyway.

He let me know that he was going to be okay and I shouldn't come home early. He was sent home later that night after his symptoms subsided.

November 5, 2014

After almost three months, Dad was finally going for the biopsy on the mass that had been scheduled. The results of Dad's blood tests showed his white blood cell count was at 32. The count was too high, putting him at risk. He was sent home with antibiotics to help clear the infection, and the biopsy had to be rescheduled for next week.

It is unbelievable that we have to continue to wait just for the test to be done, and that still won't give us any answers. The biopsy has to be sent away to a lab for analysis before we can get the results. We are all suffering from antagonizing worry. We know there is a mass, but have no idea what can be done about it.

How can the health care system move so slowly? This should have been done a long time ago and he wouldn't have needed the medication. We could have had results and had a treatment plan in place by now. Instead, we wait.

November 13, 2014

Dad was FINALLY able to get the biopsy done on the lung. During the procedure, his lung had partially deflated. He was sent home and asked to return the next day to have another x-ray taken of his lung to ensure it was not collapsed. He let us know that the procedure didn't hurt and he was okay. The test is done now, but it will take a week to ten days to get the results back from the Provincial Lab pathology.

He was taken home to rest. The waiting game continues. When he got home and looked at the papers that he had been given, he realized that someone else's appointment papers were mixed in with his paperwork. Dad had a headache tonight.

Frustrated, I contacted the Quality Assurance team to see if something could be done to try to get Dad a diagnosis and a treatment plan. It has been ten weeks and we still didn't know more than we did on September 12.

Dad had dropped to 176 pounds, felt sick all the time, was easily agitated and frustrated with the health care system. He was losing the strength needed for fighting whatever it is that he had and he wasn't able to eat a lot to get the proper nutrients for his body.

Dad returned the papers he had received for the other patient the next day when he went back for the x-ray to have his lung checked.

FEAR

November 14, 2014

Dad returned to the General Hospital in the morning. He was weak and the walk from the parking lot to his appointment had worn him out. He had the x-ray that was scheduled. It showed that his lung had returned to normal. He was very weak and not feeling very well.

When he got home, he knew something was wrong and decided he needed to get checked. Mom went with him to the medical clinic to see if he could get in to see his family doctor, but there was not an available appointment until next week. Dad was frustrated and went home to try to eat.

By 11:30 am, Dad's face turned completely white. He broke into a sweat, started vomiting, lost his balance, collapsed and became completely incoherent.

Corie was with him at the kitchen table and was able to catch him. Corie started to yell, "Mom, it's happening again!" then sent me a text message to tell me to get to Mom and Dad's house right away because there was something wrong with Dad.

I left work immediately and when I got to their house, Dad was sitting in the chair, weak, lifeless, incoherent and unable to walk. It was like he lost the ability to use his legs.

Mom and Corie managed to slowly get him maneuvered to his bed while I was on the phone trying to reach Quality Assurance. We needed answers and a plan. Fearing time was running out, I left a voicemail letting them know Dad was being brought in by ambulance, again, and we needed someone to look him right away.

When I finished the call and went to see Dad in the room, his face had a yellow colour to it. He looked terrible, incoherent and very confused.

He was upset when he was taken to hospital the last time, but we were able to communicate with him enough to convince him he needed to go to emergency. An ambulance was called and he was taken to the Pasqua Hospital.

He was talking when he was transferred to a hospital bed in a private room, but nothing was making sense. He was making comments like, "The nurses and doctors are pretend. I can see them going in and out of the same hospital rooms over and over. They can't do anything to help". He was in a bed, with his eyes closed, when he was saying it.

We tried to calm him down, but didn't have a clue what was going on. He was not acting anything like himself. In his confusion, he was convinced that he died.

We didn't know what was wrong with him, there were no test results and it felt like he was slipping away with nothing that we could do to help him. It was terrifying. He was able to talk, but he slurred his words.

We were starting to get concerned that he may have suffered a stroke. He was connected to IV for antibiotics because his white cell count was at 19.

Corie and I had left the hospital to get some things. When I got back to the hospital, Mom was upset.

While we were gone, a doctor came in to give Mom an update. The doctor told her that Dad had advanced lung cancer that spread to his brain. A CT scan was ordered to confirm the diagnosis and they were just waiting for him to go for the test. I was in shock and confused.

How could a definite diagnosis be delivered when we were just told that we had to wait for ten days for a biopsy report to come back?

Was the doctor able to get the results rushed?

How could Dad be diagnosed with brain cancer before having a CT scan?

Worry turned to panic as we sat and wait.

The first brain scan results were clear and Dad was scheduled for another CT scan with dye. Again, this scan was clear confirming that Dad did not have brain cancer.

Despite being told that he had advanced lung cancer, we still had to wait for the results of the biopsy report for another ten days to confirm the diagnosis and get treatment options.

After receiving the scan results, the next emergency doctor assigned to his case came into see him told us he planned to discharge him and send Dad home with an IV pack. We spoke to his attending physician and Dad was admitted to the hospital.

When he finally became coherent close to midnight, he said he just needed to sleep and he would feel better.

November 15, 2014

Today we found out the soonest we can expect the biopsy report will be at the end of the week. He is in a room with a very sick lady. Her family was staying with her as they prepared to say their good-byes. It's heartbreaking that the lady couldn't be in a private room with her family as they prepared for her final moments.

Putting a man that thought that he died just hours before in the same room as this family did not improve his emotional well-being either.

A curtain between the two beds did not provide a lot of privacy. It was a hard night for everyone and he wasn't able to sleep.

Dad was having difficulty eating and the smell of the hospital food made him sick. For supper, there was a slice of processed white loaf mystery meat, a scoop of dry mashed potatoes and blue jello. Dad was offered half of a brown bread sandwich that contained a slice of white mystery meat.

I can't confirm, but I think it depends on the day whether the mystery meat is called pork, turkey or chicken. I'm convinced the ingredients are the same for all three. It is disgusting.

We tried to bring Dad other food, but the smell of the hospital food would turn him off and he couldn't eat anything. It is terrifying that there are professionals that think this is good food for the healing process.

How can this food be served to our sickest citizens?

FRUSTRATION

November 16, 2014

Another day of waiting. The doctors still can't give him a diagnosis. Dad is coherent, frustrated and emotional. He can't eat or get sleep. The sleeping pills are not working to help him get rest. The thought remains, if the mass is cancer, it hasn't stopped growing. He is losing strength and weight not being able to eat. Panic is setting in, but without a diagnosis, nothing could be done.

Corie and I continued researching every possible option available for lung cancer ranging from alternative health care to the Mayo Clinic to prepare for the worst. We talked to the doctors about getting something to help him with his appetite and talked to the nurses about the food.

I moved Dad's supper tray away from his bed to the patient sink in his hospital room so it could be picked up to keep the smell as far away from him as possible and had overheard a nurse talking in the hallway, "Bed one is settled for the night, bed two died". Both parts of the sentence were said with the same tone. My mouth dropped and I was mortified. To a loved one, that one patient meant the world.

You can't walk down a hospital hallway without hearing someone on the phone, frustrated, trying to get some answers for or about their loved one.

November 17, 2014

Another stressful day. He is losing his appetite and complains the food tastes terrible regardless of what we bring. Everything tastes like metal to him.

We eventually learned that it was "thrush" on the tongue that was affecting his taste. There was medication referred to as

"Swish & Swallow" that helped. Having him eat with plastic utensils helped with reducing the metal taste.

He got a new person beside him today that listens to the TV loud and needs the lights on day and night, so he wasn't able to get rest. It was another sleepless night.

November 18, 2014

Spent most of the day researching. It's frustrating, heartbreaking and infuriating to have to wait with no answers. It's seems like the man around the tumor has been forgotten.

Family Update November 18th

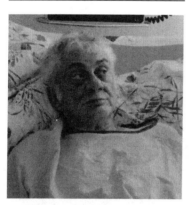

Today had several challenges. His stomach is sore, he is backed up, was not able to eat much and he hasn' t been getting sleep in the hospital.

He has a temperature of 39 degrees. The doctors believe there is infection somewhere.

They gave him anxiety medication today to try to help him relax and sleep. The pill at noon helped him to sleep for a few hours. He got another dose tonight and was sleeping within a half hour. I hope he gets some good sleep tonight and wakes up feeling better.

Frustration and fear settled in for him today and he told the doctor that he is playing with his life and he needs answers. It took a while but he was eventually more settled.

Hopefully we will get the biopsy results by Friday and a plan of attack shortly after that.

On a positive note, despite feeling crappy, he looks good. Better than he has in months, literally! He was starting to get tired from his medication and then got excited because Corie brought him an episode of Gold Rush to watch for five minutes before he nodded off.

I can promise you, he is our top priority and we are doing everything we can to keep him happy, comfortable and get answers for him as quickly as possible so he can feel better.

Taya and Tiana are the heavy weights we pull in to cheer him up and it works every time. We have a plan with every diagnosis that it could possibly be, but we need the diagnosis. They are moving as quick as humanly possible to get him answers.

November 19, 2014

We wait.

Corie was scheduled to go to Las Vegas to work on a pit crew. He didn't want to go and leave Dad, but we convinced him that he would be back before we found out anything. He went, but was worried.

Family Update November 19th AM

The doctor was in this morning. His white cell count is at 19, but is staying there despite the antibiotics he is taking. It was originally 32 a few weeks ago, but it should be at 10. The doctor is forwarding his results to a specialist to have them reviewed.

He did not sleep well last night so they are going to try something else to help him sleep better tonight. His fever broke and he was awake and feisty this morning.

We scheduled him a haircut and he is expecting some visitors this afternoon.

Family Update November 19th PM

Dad had a pain free day and just wants sleep. Hopefully tonight will be the night he gets a good rest, fingers crossed.

He didn't have much of an appetite today, but he did eat. His stomach is feeling better and he is making plans for things he wants to do in the spring.

There is a hairdresser at the hospital and he got a nice haircut today!

Corie flew to Vegas so he can work on a pit crew for a friend of his that is racing in the National Street Race Car championship finals. We are all excited to be able to watch the videos. It will be a great distraction and will give Dad something fun to think about to pass the time until he gets some answers.

ANGER

November 20, 2014

Still waiting for a diagnosis.

<u>Family Update November 20th</u>

Nap time is a hot commodity. Dad was sleeping when we got to the hospital this morning at ten and now he is dozing off again. We have the lights off and Mom is sitting quietly with him now. We hope he sleeps until tomorrow morning. He is in such desperate need of a good rest which seems like mission impossible in the hospital.

I heard a nurse in the hallway say to a patient in another room, "If you need something and no one is listening, ask God, he is always available".

It was the most honest comment we have heard in weeks.

November 22, 2014

I sent a letter to Quality Assurance:

Please find attached a copy of the information we had discussed on the phone last week. Allen Triffo has agreed to allow access to his files. A copy of his experiences since November 13th have been documented and attached.

Three months has been a long time for him to know that he has aggressive cancer without a treatment plan. Is there any possible way to get answers for him rushed?

It is our understanding that the biopsy was only taken of the lung, not the tumor, and another biopsy may be required, which could take another two weeks to get the results.

Without a diagnosis, treatment is impossible. Is a PET scan in Saskatoon an option?

Attachment sent to Quality Assurance – Allen Triffo

November 13, 2014:

Allen Triffo had a lung biopsy at the General Hospital followed by two x-rays before being sent home. His lung deflated a little so they asked him to return the next morning for another x-ray to ensure the lung was okay. Allen was sent home with discharge papers that included another patient's appointment.

November 14, 2014:

Just after lunch, Allen Triffo was transported to the Pasqua Hospital by ambulance after vomiting, breaking into a sweat, becoming very pale, unable to walk and incoherent. He has been vomiting for the past three weeks and unable to keep food down.

The first emergency doctor told him that he suspected Allen had aggressive lung cancer that spread to the brain and ordered two CT scans to confirm the diagnosis. The CT scans showed that the brain was clear. Allen did not have brain cancer.

Allen remained disorientated and incoherent until the evening. The second doctor had suggested that he could be discharged with IV. He was admitted after speaking with the attending physician.

Another emergency doctor prescribed a prostate pill and it is uncertain why. He has had never had medication for the prostate before.

It is November 22, 2014 and Allen has been doctoring for this situation since the beginning of September. We still do not have a diagnosis or a treatment plan.

Allen is currently at the Pasqua Hospital. With being told on multiple occasions that it is aggressive cancer, despite not having a diagnosis since the beginning of September.

It is frustrating that no treatment can be done. I suspect rapid cancer does not stop to wait for doctors and test results for ten weeks. It's growing and he is losing the strength he needs to fight.

Family Update November 23rd

Yesterday Mom managed to get Dad to go for a walk around the ward.

We are hoping the biopsy report will be back before the end of the week as an hour feels like a week to Dad with all this waiting.

The doctor had sedated him and he got a little rest for the first time last night. The best time to plan a visit is at meal time as he will be awake. He tries to sleep the rest of the time.

We just found out the CT scan for his stomach came back clear. There is no stomach cancer. That is the only test result we have got back this week.

We will take the good news.

This is what waiting looks like.

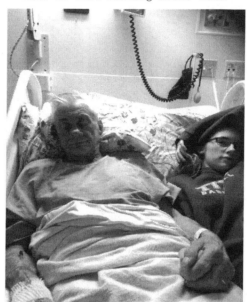

November 24, 2014

A year ago today, Dad and Corie were watching the 101st Grey Cup in the box seats at Taylor Field. The Saskatchewan Roughriders beat the Hamilton Tiger Cats to win the Grey Cup championship on home turf.

It is crazy how much can change in a year!

Family Update November 24th

The doctor has finally figured out something to make him sleep at night. That is success.

We will take the win!

DENIAL

November 25, 2014

Today we met with the chemo oncologist. Dad was very weak and we wheeled him down to the Allan Blair clinic where we met with a pharmacist and the registration desk.

We proceeded to wait in the waiting room for almost an hour. Dad was so weak, that sitting up for a few minutes in his room usually exhausts him. The situation was not ideal.

When we finally met with the oncologist, Dad put out his hand to introduce himself. The doctor didn't seem overly interested in talking to us. Every question we asked, he shrugged his shoulders and said, "I don't know" or "well". The entire appointment went that way. After weeks of desperately wanting answers, it was like Dad didn't matter. To that doctor, he was just another patient. To us, he was the center of our world. Watching him being treated that way was disgusting.

We asked about the alternative to chemo pill and he had no idea what we were talking about. When Dad asked about an approximate time for life expectancy, the doctor responded with, "I've met you for three minutes, I don't have a crystal ball to tell you how much time you have left." That is the only comment during the appointment that was appreciated. Another oncologist was requested.

We knew he wasn't strong enough for chemo, but we were told that it was up to the radiologist to provide the options.

Family Update November 25th

Dad spent more time sitting up today, he looks good and is looking forward to having a good sleep.

November 26, 2014

The biopsy results came back showing that it was cancer on the outside of the lung. Operating was not possible due to the location of the tumor. Chemo and radiation will be the only options. Not the news we were hoping for, but we were prepared for it.

Family Update November 26th

We understand that everyone is concerned and worried.

The biopsy results have been received and a treatment plan is being worked on, but we do not know available options yet. He is not receiving any treatment at this time.

Please try to understand that this is a very difficult time for Dad and the information we know is for him to share. We are respecting his privacy and letting him tell others on his own, if he chooses to.

He is still in the same room at the Pasqua Hospital. His medications are letting him get more sleep, he is able to eat a little more and his strength is improving, for that we are grateful.

The six of us are facing every challenge together and right now 100% of our energy is focused on lifting his spirits, making sure he is comfortable and we are quickly preparing for the fight of our lives.

We feel your love, support and concern and it is greatly appreciated.

BARGAINING

November 27, 2014

We had met with the radiology oncologist to see what the options for treatment were. Dad is weak and unable to eat.

Option 1 | Take six weeks of radiology. This could provide 20% chance of survival, according to statistics, but is not recommended. He could get weaker, ill and dehydrated. Once treatment starts it has to be completed and cannot be done again. There is a possibility of permanent damage to his lung.

Option 2 | Three weeks of radiation with no chance of killing the cancer. It could improve quality of life for up to two years.

Option 3 | Do nothing.

Dad is a fighter, but the risks of the first option were too great with him in the state his is in right now. The decision made is what we have to live with. There is no turning back to choose another option later. Radiation can only be administered once to the same spot and the full treatment has to be completed.

If we would have had the results eight weeks prior when he was still able to eat and had strength, it would have been easy to choose the first option. It was devastating to have that option taken away because he was forced to wait so long for a diagnosis. Blaming the healthcare system at this point wouldn't solve anything. It was too late. The only thing we could do was support Dad in whatever decision he made.

When asked what he wanted to do, he didn't want the option that could permanently damage his lungs. He shrugged his shoulders to the second option. The final option was do nothing, and he just said, "Okay".

The radiology oncologist sat there for a moment. We all thought that he had decided to refuse treatment and opted for doing nothing. She was about to get up and Dad asked her, "Well, what are you going to do? You have to do something."

After some thought, and reviewing all the options again, we all agreed the middle option was the only thing his body would be able to tolerate in his existing state. It was such a hard decision to have to choose delaying the inevitable. We are just hoping that he has some good time left.

Arrangements are being made to get him in for treatment as soon as possible, but trying to get his strength up and make sure he is hydrated are top priorities. He is being scheduled for sixteen rounds of radiation. His last treatment will be on Christmas Eve.

We heard many doctors say that there isn't a cure. My thoughts are that all living things have an expiry date and no one is guaranteed tomorrow. If you add an apostrophe and a space, the word impossible changes to I'm possible. We were doing everything we could to help him enjoy his good minutes.

Dad always said, "When your number is up, it is up" and "Expect the worst, and hope for the best". His mentality was if he was meant to survive, he would. His body would live until it died. It's that simple.

Family Update November 30th
Dad has been tired but was able to watch the Grey Cup today. He was cheering for Hamilton. What a close game.

We have him set up watching Gold Rush and old westerns which will hopefully help pass the time until Wednesday.

December 1, 2014

Frustration was running high when his meal was delivered today. It is so important that he eats so that he can get some strength and we cannot get a dietician to come in to help.

Today, yellow and cream are the colour of the menu. Juice full of sugar, instant pudding and pasta with mystery cheese for a guy that has been backed up for weeks.

I struggle to understand how a plate full of sugar and processed food, with no fruit or vegetables, can be served to our sickest citizens with the expectation of helping them get well.

On top of what was being served, how it was cooked was another issue. In the hallway, I heard a doctor make a comment that it takes as much effort to prepare food to taste good as it does to make it taste terrible. I agree.

I challenge the minister of health and premier to take a visit to the hospital and enjoy the food given to the patients. If they are healthy before visiting the hospital, I'm willing to bet they would feel ill before leaving. Gross.

This is what taxpayers paying for? If it is because of money, then priorities need to be reviewed. There is a multi-million dollar stadium being built right beside the hospital that can't afford to feed their patients decent meals. We looked out the window and watched it being built while he was in the hospital.

Whole, non-processed foods, were rarely included on the trays. It didn't matter what we tried to feed him, his taste buds were off and everything tasted terrible, but the smell of the hospital food was making a bad situation worse.

Even if we brought him different food, he could smell his neighbours' food and it would make him sick. We eventually gave up on nutrient dense food and settled for trying to get anything that we could into him in an effort to help him get some strength back.

Family Update December 1st

Dad slept most of the day but finally ate some supper. Ham and perogies with carrots, which is the first edible meal (with the exception of cream of wheat two mornings) that they have served to him in a while. Hoping it helps him get some energy so he feels like walking tomorrow.

Family Update December 2nd

Dad got a cinnamon bun from Nickys Café today and he really enjoyed it. He got a cabbage roll, chicken, head cheese and cottage cheese.

We have a tiny cooler by his bed that we fill with ice that drinks can sit on so they will stay cold.

HE ATE!!! That is a great day.

We got smart today and started playing old country music for him and he is enjoying it. It calms him down.

He will be starting treatment tomorrow at 2:40 pm, FINALLY! We are all hoping that it helps him a little so he can get energy to live some good minutes.

SADNESS

December 3, 2014

We went to radiation with Dad today and got to talk to a dietician in the Allan Blair Clinic. She will be contacting the dietician on the unit to see if we can get some food for him.

He is not wanting to get out of bed anymore, feels crappy, says all the food tastes like burnt plastic and he is agitated.

I sent a reply to the Quality Assurance team:

Allen Triffo is still in the Pasqua Hospital. His diagnosis is advanced small cell lung cancer. Due to his deteriorated state he is unable to take the radiation treatments that would've given him a twenty percent chance of survival, according to statistics. This would've been an option had he not had to wait for three months trying to work through the red tape of the health care system. Instead, he has had his doctors tell him to get his affairs in order and that there is no cure for what he has.

His hospital doctor had to call pathology every day last week to get the biopsy results and had requested that he be notified as soon as the results were available. It is my understanding that pathology did not provide the information to him as he requested and it was another two days of unnecessary waiting.

The nurses have been calling the dietician every day for over a week to try to get Allen Triffo some decent food.
The dietician was supposed to see Allen eleven days ago and still has not arrived.

He is receiving things for supper like a slice of processed meat with a scoop of mashed potatoes (an entirely white plate of food without so much as a vegetable), blue jello, inedible dried up pork slices, over cooked carrots and world's tiniest meat balls covered in an inedible sauce. How are sick people supposed to heal when they don't have proper food? Something has to be done with the hospital food! Inedible food in a hospital is unacceptable.

Why is the dietician not coming to see my Dad? It shouldn't take eleven days with countless calls from the nurses.

I highly recommend that the minister of health and premier sit in a hospital bed and be served breakfast, lunch and supper every day for a week. In that time, they would have the opportunity to get a good idea what is being served for meals here and be forced to listen to what families have to deal with.

Allen starts radiation today, but my Mom had received a call at home from radiology on Monday and the person asked for Jeff. I'm guessing that someone was working with two files in radiology and the wrong phone number was recorded in the wrong file because the caller verified the number she was calling was the correct number. How can that happen? How is information getting cross referenced? It is the second time in a month.

How can we be sure that we even have the right diagnosis if he is being sent home with the wrong discharge papers and, the simple things like contact information, isn't being recorded properly?

More seriously, he was given prostate medication in emergency when he wasn't supposed to be. How can there be this many mix ups? What is being done about it?

Doctors and nurses have to spend more time running after people that should be supporting them help patients than is humanly comprehendible. It's a waste of their time. It is truly embarrassing to be a Saskatchewan taxpayer. I'll be at the hospital for the rest of the week.

Family Update December 3rd

First day of radiation was today mid-afternoon. He didn't eat today and has slept the majority of the time. Hoping for a better day tomorrow.

When Dad wanted water, he liked it freezing cold. I had two containers that were filled with water and frozen solid daily. I would take one up in the morning when I would take Mom up to the hospital to visit him and another at night. He would drink water as the ice melted.

Family Update December 4th

Another very quiet day.

Tried to get him to watch a John Wayne movie at supper time, but he listened to it instead. He was in pain today and isn't at all interested in food. He slept most of the day away.

He likes listening to the radio and we keep it playing so he taps his toes and fingers. That is the most we got for exercise out of him today with the exception of one trip to the bathroom.

Family Update December 5th

He was awake for a little bit today and asked for a coffee! That's a first in a week. He ate a little at lunch and supper but at least it was a little. Corie was able to get him to exercise some today!

We will take the small wins.

DEPRESSION

December 6, 2014

Today was a terrible day. Dad had no idea what was going on. He was hallucinating and seeing things.

When he would talk to us he would get frustrated because we couldn't see what he saw. There were times he didn't even know who we were. What he was saying was so strange, it was funny.

He wanted a muffin. When I asked him what kind, he got frustrated and said one like he was already eating. Eventually we just went along with whatever he said because his thought patterns were lasting about 30 seconds at a time before switching to something new.

He was making actions like he was eating in his sleep, tried to pull out his tongue because he thought it was something strange in his mouth and was attempting to pull a banana out of his arm. He looks and acts hungry, but he must be filling up on imaginary food because we can't get him to eat anything real.

Poor Tiana was heartbroken and devastated. Going home tonight I felt completely deflated and sure that there is no hope.

Family Update December 6th

It was a terrible day. Dad is hallucinating and is completely incoherent. He was not awake for more than an hour the whole day. They started IV to try to help with dehydration. He talks in his sleep, but did not know who Tiana was tonight.

We are all completely exhausted, broken hearted and going to bed praying for a better day tomorrow.

Family Update December 7th
Today was the same. Dad is more coherent when others are around.

Family Update December 8th

Dad had fun talking about the good 'ol days with company today and it was good to see him laugh. He had a better day and his confusion has decreased dramatically, but still has moments.

We are still having problems trying to get him to eat anything because nothing tastes right and his stomach is easily upset.

Family Update December 9th

Today he had a much better day. He was able to eat breakfast, had a shower and a good sleep this afternoon. His appetite still isn' t great and his stomach still hurts, but we are hoping to get something to help with that.

Radiation is scheduled for 10:10 am tomorrow.

December 10, 2014

A year ago I had purchased a book called, "Never Leave Your Wingman" and finally read it before going to sleep. There is some renewed hope that we will have more good minutes with Dad and the book gave me a fun idea.

Dad was constantly told, "There isn't a cure", "There is no hope", and "Get your affairs in order". A new doctor would come in assuming a new diagnosis based on symptoms, rather than test results. It was frustrating.

Holocaust survivors used their imaginations to escape from the traumatic situations to get a degree of separation from the torture that they were being subjected to. They used their imaginations to create good minutes rather than focusing on their existing reality. Why is it different for terminal patients?

Why can't those patients use their imagination to be healthy and happy rather than doing a countdown to their last minute, which is unknown anyway?

They are living, why do they have to be reminded that they are dying before they take their last breath? Dad's affairs were in order, I'm not sure what else can be expected.

If you look on the internet, articles explain anxiety is caused from looking into the future and depression is from focusing on the past. Why does anxiety have to be added to an already stressful situation?

I don't have a PhD, but when terminal illness is mentioned, it is clear that days are numbered. There are only two options: enjoy every moment and cherish what time you have left or be scared, sad and miserable.

As Dad was battling cancer and facing his mortality, teenagers were being lost to car accidents, suicides and violence.

The truth is that everyone should be enjoying every moment because life does not guarantee anyone tomorrow.

Family Update December 10th

Dad had a very busy and great day. He was feeling good before his radiation this morning, had an X-ray and three meetings.

He got some good sleep since early this afternoon. Hoping for another good day tomorrow.

December 11, 2014

It is time to add a little humor to the days.

Today I had a full day at work, but found enough time to get all the supplies I needed to get my plan in motion!

Family Update December 11th

Dad has not been feeling well today and eating is still a constant battle. We have decided to add a little excitement to the room.

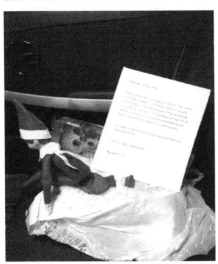

Look who is Dad's newest visitor! He will likely find him later tonight when he wakes up for a drink. Lol.

You should see what this little man has planned for the next little while!

Hopefully it will cause him to laugh a little. Radiation is at 2:40 pm tomorrow.

The note says:

Dear Mr. Allen Triffo

Please allow me to introduce myself. My name is Elf on the Shelf. I am Santa's helper usually sent to spy on children to see if they are being naughty or nice, but I am making an exception to come visit you until I have to head back to the North Pole to help Santa on Christmas Eve. I'm hoping to find you some food that is a little less crappy.

See you again tomorrow.

Naught E. Elf

Family Update December 12th AM

Dad had radiation today at 11:20 am. While he was at his appointment the elf was up to no good again!

The note says:

AL HELP!

Look at what they did to my nuts.

Naught E. Elf

Family Update December 12th PM

His stomach and head are sore. We still struggle to get him to eat. He is living on chocolate milk.

A small piece of banana and a little honey is what we managed today, which is a relief, because yesterday the wrong honey was at the hospital. Elf stepped up and helped out.

The note reads:

Hey Al,

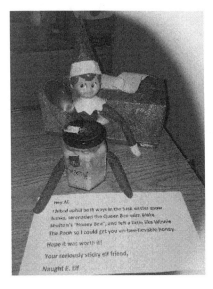

I hiked uphill both ways in the Sask winter snow banks, serenaded the Queen Bee with Blake Shelton's "Honey Bee", and felt a little like Winnie The Pooh so I could get you un-bee-lievable honey.

Hope it was worth it!

Your seriously sticky elf friend,

Naught E. Elf

Family Update December 13

Exciting news this morning! Dad woke up hungry! That is the first time in ten days!!!

He was able to eat the egg whites of an egg, three orange pieces, 3/4 of a breakfast sausage, chocolate milk, a few hash browns, a couple of teaspoons of soup and a sip of coffee into him! That is huge success!!! He did get a couple bites of a cookie and a candy down too.

Elf is also making an effort.

The note reads:

Hey Big Al,

We are all out of the tall bread, so I brought you the short stuff.

Try it out!

Naught E. Elf

Family Update December 14th

Dad slept 99% of today. Eating and drinking was not an option. Elf could not convince him to drink juice either.

His head and throat were sore and he had heartburn.

The hallucinations have returned. He thought there was a snake on his ceiling and the room filled with moths, beetles and flies.

Radiation is scheduled for 10:10 am tomorrow.

When Dad was working, he got the nickname of "Assassin" because of a boxer that he reminded people of.

The note read:

Dear Assassin,

Can you please take care of the juice for me? I want it gone and I think you are the man for the job.

Bottoms up!

Naught E. Elf

Family Update December 15th

Day 31 in hospital. He finished his ninth treatment today. The only thing he is interested in is water. His throat is very sore. He is experiencing less chest pain. We managed to get him into the shower today.

Visitors brought fruit cake today. That is gold!

Elf made him a little something today.

He is starting to look to see what elf is up to, but it is clear he is more excited about fruit cake than elf's stale donuts.

The note reads:

Hey Triffo,

How about a donut? I just made them fresh last month.
They are a little dry, but should be ok if you have them
with a little milk.

Enjoy!

Naught E. Elf

December 16, 2014

*Tonight I had a shower, wrapped myself in a towel and just sat
on my bed for a moment to think.*

*I grabbed a glass of water from beside my bed to take a sip,
laid my head back and closed my eyes for a moment to rest. I
woke up eight hours later in the same position with the glass
still in my hand and contacts still in my eyes!*

I got up and got ready for another day. We are all exhausted.

Today's note reads:

Ok Triff:

I was walking the halls and
heard a doctor say, "pee on
it". That works for
jellyfish bites you know.

Maybe it will help with your
taste buds too.

All ears,

Naught E. Elf

From Quality Assurance

Hi Calynda,

From your e-mail I see that you are continuing to be disappointed by the responsiveness and by the services. I see that there is a response from the emergency doctor. I am attaching it to this e-mail. He is the first physician who saw your Dad in ER. I believe that his response will answer some of your questions.

In regard to your concern with the prostate medication your father was prescribed, I need to follow up on this. This was another ER physician.

Thanks for clarifying that it was on Nov. 13th, that your Dad was sent home with someone else's information. I will send this to Radiology for their review and response. I do hope that your father is receiving good care.

Letter from ER Physician

Quality Assurance,

I have not reviewed the chart, but I remember Mr. Triffo and his presentation to the Emergency Department. I will lead you through my thought processes that night and if it is sufficient to answer the family's concerns, I will leave it at that. If not, I will review his chart and answer them based on the review.

Mr. Triffo presented to Emergency with a change in his behavior and level of consciousness. It sounded to me like it may have been what we call a complex partial seizure. It is a seizure that presents as a sudden onset of confusion and strange behavior.

Mr. Triffo is a smoker and had also had a biopsy of a lung mass. In a person who smokes and has a lung mass, lung cancer is obviously something we worry about.

Then, when he presents with what I think is a new seizure, I need to also think that he may have cancer that has spread to the brain. To diagnose this, we need to get a CT scan of his brain.

Unfortunately, if I remember correctly, it was after the CT technician had gone home, so the CT had to wait until the next day. I passed my concerns on to the day doctor advising him of what my concerns were and why I was getting the CT.

I was also very clear in my discussion with the family exactly what my concerns were and why I needed to get the CT done. I went home, went to bed and when I awoke, I phoned the day doctor as I wanted to know the results. I was very relieved to hear that he did not have any evidence of a brain tumor and the doctor also advised me that he had a more in depth conversation with Mr. Triffo's family about how he and they were managing at home. After that conversation, he thought it was best to admit Mr. Triffo.

I would like to explain my thought processes and specifically address Mr. Triffo's family's concerns regarding his care up to the point that I was involved. Again, Mr. Triffo is a smoker and had just had a lung biopsy. Lung cancer is a very high possibility. I did say that lung cancer can be very aggressive and that is true. Sadly, in my career, I have seen many people die of lung cancer.

With his presentation, I was honestly very concerned that he had cancer that had spread to his brain. In telling the family this, I was not trying to unnecessarily worry his family, but I was trying to be honest.

They may not believe me, but I have had many instances in my career where I have had similar conversations with families, have been correct in my suspicions, and have had families thank me as they have had time to prepare for receiving news of a bad diagnosis.

As well, I like to explain to patients exactly why I order the tests I do. That way, when someone comes to take a patient for a test, both the patient and their family knows why they are getting the test done.

Although I did not mean to cause Mr. Triffo and his family unnecessary worry and I am grateful that there was no evidence of cancer in his brain, I was only try to lead them through my thought processes and prepare them for what I thought was causing his health problem. I also understand, that until they discovered that his CT scan was normal, I did cause unnecessary worry, and I apologize for that.

As for further treatment of the lung mass, that must await the biopsy results. The biopsy is read by a pathologist and I am sorry, but I have no control over the speed at which biopsies are examined. I would like to say, however, that until the biopsy is examined, we do not know what the mass is. It might be cancer or it might not. If it is cancer, it might be aggressive or it might not. I was only giving the example that, if what I thought was a seizure was caused by a brain tumor that would suggest an aggressive cancer. A cancer that has spread, in his case, from the lung. Again, I apologize for the miscommunication.

Mr. Triffo's care extended from my shift into another shift. Had I been involved in his care from start to finish, I would have explained this to him and his family. I would have explained that he does not have cancer in his brain and to know what the lung mass is will require interpretation of the biopsy by a pathologist. I should have asked the doctor to explain this. Instead, I just reviewed Mr. Triffo's history and physical with the doctor, what I thought the diagnosis was and why I was getting the CT scan. The doctor wouldn't have known that I had left and given the family the impression that Mr. Triffo definitely has metastatic cancer.

Lastly, to address why he was put on any medication, I will have to defer to the physician that wrote the orders. I cannot comment on that as my shift had ended and I had gone home. I hope this helps lead the family through my thoughts that night to help them get an understanding of why I said the things I said. It was out of concern and honesty. It was certainly not meant to cause any pain or harm. If you, Mr. Triffo and his family are happy with knowing my thoughts from that night, I will consider the matter closed. If they are not happy and have further questions for me, please let me know.

That letter was never responded to.

A doctors words are powerful. Physicians are usually expected to provide a quick fix with a pill or surgical procedure for every ailment their patients have. Psychic 101 is not included in their medical training, but they are expected to estimate life expectancies as well.

Doctors are well educated, deserve respect and have access to many ways to help those that are ill; however, they are still human. There are times that mistakes will be made. Like anyone else, they are influenced to react based on what they know and have experience with. Unfortunately, this doctor had witnessed these symptoms before with other patients and expected Dad to have the same diagnosis.

We knew there was a possibility of cancer when Dad was told that there was a mass on his lung in September. In 2009, when he had lost his brother to lung cancer, Dad was with him through the journey and by his side when he took his last breath. He knew what lung cancer could do. Unfortunately, our family wasn't a stranger to the dreaded disease either. Like the doctor, those memories were already in his thoughts while he waited.

The doctor's suspicions were wrong and having the doctor share this information did not improve Dad's emotional well-being or his families. The stress and worry were intensified knowing nothing could be done without the confirmed diagnosis. All Dad required and wanted were the facts so that he could process the information, figure out a plan, and find the best course of action he was willing to take.

This doctors' heart was in the right place, but I do not agree with diagnosing based on suspicion. Everyone is unique. It is understood doctors do not want to give "false" hope so they can suggest to patients to get their affairs in order.

Shouldn't everyone have their affairs in order? People can choke on their lunch or get in an accident. Those people do not get the opportunity to prepare for anything. They live every minute as a good minute, without having to look death in the face for an extended period of time.

There are statistics that are used to determine the prognosis with terminal illness. If 100% of the people at one point died of an illness, until one person conquered it, the survival statistics for that illness would be zero. The minute someone beats the illness, the statistics change. Statistics give an idea of survival rates, but they are not a guarantee.

Until you have been through a similar journey, step-by-step, with someone very close to you, it's impossible to explain the lengths that you would go to ease your loved one's pain, have them comfortable, get them to eat or let them spend another day doing whatever they want to.

It changes who you are and thought processes. Previous experience already had its impact on us, so my reactions were likely different than most people's perspectives.

FRUSTRATION

Family Update December 17th

Dad is back to hallucinating and spent most of the day sleeping.

Tomorrow is another day.

To Quality Assurance

I just got up to the hospital to visit my Dad and apparently another female doctor was in to see him this morning to tell him that there is no hope. Is there any way to get these doctors to quit coming in sharing their, "you are going to die" opinions with him?

Quite frankly, if he dies tomorrow, I'd rather see him die with hope than to have him robbed of it every time we turn around. Everyone is going to die, thanks for the memo.

How about I gather a group of cancer survivors that were told that they were going to be dead in six months and they are now cancer free, can they look at them and say there is no hope too?

Since they are so experienced, can they tell me when I am going to die while they are playing God? An apology to my Dad from these doctors would be appreciated. Last I checked their Ph.D did not grant them God status.

Every time we get him to the point that he starts to feel better, a new doctor comes in and shares their doom and gloom opinion and we are right back at square one. It's ridiculous.

NOTE: The doctors causing frustration in the Quality Assurance emails were not Dad's regular physicians and they were not aware of his whole medical history and situation. There were several doctors that worked with Dad, and the majority of them were amazing. These letters represented the minority.

From Quality Assurance

Before I sent the e-mail to the Department Head of Family Medicine, I decided that I'd best confirm that it was the attending.

I am told that the attending has not been up today and it is a male. The charge nurse thought that it was an Oncologist but I didn't recognize the name, so have put in a call for a new listing of the oncologists.

If it is an oncologist I will contact the client representative at cancer services and forward your letter to her as we don't have any mandate with cancer services. If you aren't okay with this please let me know.

To Quality Assurance

We know that his radiology oncologist was in to see him this morning and it wasn't her that said anything because we were with him when she was there.

I know there was a nurse, she was up yesterday, but I don't think it was her because he said he didn't see this new doctor before.

I know that there is a female doctor on the unit, but she isn't Dad's doctor, so I don't think she would see him. His Oncologist is male who I had talked about in a previous email.

How do we know who went into his room?

From Quality Assurance

I'm stumped. Could you ask your Dad's nurse? It was the charge nurse that I asked.

To Quality Assurance

I'm not certain who the nurse was yesterday. The only female doctor on the ward that I've seen isn't the one that came into the room. I'm stumped too.

What I can tell you is the attending doctor did come into talk to my Mom in the afternoon and told her that the cancer has spread to his throat and recommended we change his Living Will to DNR.

Please let me know what tests my Dad has undergone that are concrete evidence that his cancer has indeed spread to his throat and that it is not the tumor pressing on the esophagus which was determined by the CT scans that we discussed with the radiology oncologist at noon.

It is my understanding another CT scan has to be ordered in January to determine if the radiation helped as there is swelling around the area where the tumor is.

Just to recap ...

He was diagnosed with pneumonia in September by his family doctor. It took us until November 21st to have the biopsy report show that it was stage 3 lung cancer.

On November 14th he was diagnosed with seizures, lung cancer and brain cancer by an emergency doctor based on his assumptions a week before any biopsy report was received.

There was no brain cancer and he has never been diagnosed with seizures. The tumor is outside his lung pressing on his esophagus from what has been explained to us, although it is coming from the lung.

He was put on a prostate pill by another emergency doctor for reasons that we still do not understand.

The medical oncologist treated Allen like he was a waste of time and that we were interrupting his day during the two hour appointment, completely disinterested in answering questions and didn't tell us anything other than he doesn't have a crystal ball so he doesn't know how long Allen has to live.

He was told there was no cure or hope by multiple doctors including a mystery woman doctor.

The attending doctor has diagnosed him with throat cancer as of today and asked us to change a DNR based on what?

Allen choked yesterday, if company wasn't there, Mom was certain he would've choked to death. Mom told the attending doctor about it and his comment was, in his condition that would've been okay. His personal opinion was not appreciated. That is the wife of a patient, how can a comment like that be considered professional? When Mom had rang for a nurse for help, the nurse stood at the end of the bed and said, oh he is just choking and left the room. Is it my Mom's job to help him in this situation or was she just supposed to leave him choke while she watched her husband die?

I want someone with some test results that can speak to us and let us know EXACTLY what we are dealing with because I think the radiology oncologist is the one that should know. She is so good with him when she talks to him. The other doctors are telling us something completely different. My mother does not need to be dealing with this added stress.

I would like to let these physicians know that they have made this experience completely miserable for the man lying in that hospital bed and for the family that loves him. No more educated guesses are required. I promise the facts of his prognosis are bad enough. The educated guessing and assumptions are just adding unnecessary worry and making a terrible situation unbearable, not to mention adding to the depression and anxiety for Dad. Unless there is a CT Scan, PET scan, or some other report/test that provides concrete evidence of his condition to back up their opinions, we've got all the educated memos based on assumptions that we can tolerate.

He knows he is dying, from way more things than what the test results show, depending on what doctor he has had on any given week. The point has been driven home! Let it also be known, every other person living is also dying. Until someone certified as God is able to let us know the date, time, and condition as to which Allen Triffo is dying from, please don't continue to make a terrible situation worse.

We will continue to help him have good minutes until he quits breathing and make decisions based on facts from the results of any tests that are done.

A sincere thank you to his regular doctors and incredible nurses on the unit that, despite the prognosis, make Dad comfortable and provide him with peace with what they have to tell him. They provide facts, without robbing him of his good minutes, compared to adding anxiety, depression and misery for whatever time he has left.

***

Taya had a school project where she was assigned a computerized life like baby that she had to take care of for 24 hours.

The baby would cry, needed to be fed, required a diaper change and Taya was graded on how quickly she responded.

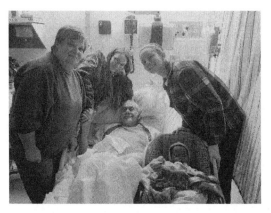

The "baby" had to be taken up to the hospital with us. She got to the hospital lobby and ordered some food before having to take it out of the baby carrier to attend to it. It attracted some attention.

We went to visit Dad and there was a family photo taken.

Family Update December 17th

Day 32 in hospital and day 10 of radiation.

He isn't having a lot of fun but he was concerned when I was setting up elf that he was going to fall over.

Dr. Elf is reading:

The Guide to Fixing Big Al.

The note reads:

Hey Al,

Just doing a little research here. I'll let you know if I figure anything out!

Dr. Naught E. Elf

Dad was somewhat amused by elf's book.

Corie interrupted Naught E. Elf today and he took a tumble right into the garbage can.

Poor thing is a true patient in the hospital room. He cannot even use the facilities without being bugged.

Elf found the perfect balloon for Dad. It says, Eat, drink and be crabby!

The note reads:

Triffo,

Why is everyone up in the air around here?

Keep Chillin

Naught E Elf

December 18, 2014

Dad was sleeping when we got to the hospital this morning, but woke up long enough to tell us that his family doctor was up and all he really said is things have to start changing around here.

I spoke with Quality Assurance to try to get things settled and received a few calls from the cancer clinic to get matters straightened out there as well, then I got a call from Mom.

Another doctor on the floor, that was not Dad's doctor, came into talk to her and was telling her that he could go home because he was in an acute bed and he couldn't stay there. After speaking with the resource nurse, it was understood that Dad would remain where he was until he is able to eat, drink and function. We also requested a feeding tube as he hasn't been able to eat a meal in over three weeks.

Dad had asked for bologna, nature's rye bread, keens mustard and mushroom soup for supper. It isn't what we want to see him eat, but it beats him starving to death and if he was willing to eat it, we were willing try anything. A quick trip was made to Safeway to get the goods and the soup was purchased from Robin's donuts. Swish and swallow, to help with thrush, was given an hour before to try to help with his taste.

Excited that he was wanting to finally eat, we got everything set up on his table when he let me know that I got the wrong harvest bologna! I bought the blue package instead of the red one. This was a crisis. He was disappointed and his cravings didn't last very long. There was only a small window of opportunity before they passed.

I rushed back to Safeway to make the exchange. When I got the correct package back to the hospital, he sat up and ate one slice of the bologna, but something wasn't smelling right in the room. The burnt plastic smell was back.

He took one spoonful of the soup, gagged and it all came up. Thankfully he tried another slice of bologna and he was able to keep that down, then went back to sleep. When he swallows he gets extreme pain in the back of his head so it is very hard for him to get any food down.

Family Update December 18th

Thanks to the Saskatchewan Health care system for two full days of hell. We have been working at getting Dad a feeding tube and spend most of the time refusing to let Dad be discharged from the hospital. He has not been able to eat a decent meal in three weeks and is not mobile.

Having the new doctor of the day coming in diagnosing him with a different type of cancer based on assumptions has really lifted everyone's spirits, or maybe that is our blood pressure. It is hard to say.

The radiologists and oncologists that Dad had were the best that we could have hoped for. The nurses did their very best to provide Allen with whatever was required to try to keep him comfortable and remain in good spirits.

Those doctors and nurses hold a very special place in our hearts. It's to help these health care providers get the proper diagnostic tools and support, so they can better assist their patients, that this book is being written.

Again, they are not to be confused with the few doctors that were not familiar with his health history and doing what they thought was best to help, while pushing our patience past the breaking point.

December 19, 2014

Great news! Today the radiology oncologist was assigned as his doctor during his stay in the hospital. She is going on holidays though, so another oncologist has been assigned to him while she is away. That doctor is amazing too. What a relief. Dad was awake and a little confused.

They are going to be giving him a steroid pill to help give him strength, eat and help with the inflammation in the throat.

Christmas has been the furthest thing from my mind. After work, I managed to take enough time to run to the dollar store, grab a pretend Christmas tree and some gift bags to put presents in. A good enough Christmas is organized so Tiana won't be deprived.

From Quality Assurance:

I have not had a response from Emergency in regard to the prostate medication but another representative will send that to you when it comes. I know that these are not your main concerns right now but I want to forward them to you so you have them when you have time to read them. I hope that they are helpful. The forms from Medical Imaging are very hard to read and the manager's conclusion is on the last page.

I see from the data base that a radiology oncologist is now your Dad's attending doctor. I surely trust that this will improve communication and care planning for your Dad.

Now I have not done anything with the letter you sent about the doctor who talked with your Dad on Dec. 17th other than send it to the Department Head for Family Medicine. Our usual process, when we get a physician concern is to send it to the physician with a copy to the Department Head and request that the physician write a letter of response. The doctor is a locum with Palliative Care.

Dietician Response:

I am writing to you in response the concerns raised by you and your family to the Client Representative related to dietitian services during your father's current hospital stay on his unit at Pasqua Hospital.

I would like to begin by acknowledging the disappointing experience your family has had regarding the quality of nutrition care and meal service during your hospital stay and I apologize for not meeting your expectations. Thank you for taking the time to inform us of your concerns so that we can take steps to prevent similar occurrences in the future.

I was able to review Mr. Triffo's medical record from his current stay. The care staff first documented a request to speak to a dietitian about better food choices on the evening of November 26.

At this time, it was not documented if a call was placed to the dietitian and a dietitian consult was not entered into the computerized system.

A further request to see a dietitian was documented by the care aid on November 30, at which time the care aid indicated that she had left a message. The first documented visit by a Registered Dietitian was on December 4. The dietitian indicated that she had been contacted by the dietitian at Allan Blair Cancer Centre (ABCC) who had met with your father on December 3.

I have spoken to the dietitian responsible for providing nutrition care to the unit. She reported that prior to being contacted by the dietitian from Alan Blair Cancer Centre, she had not received a consult to see Mr. Triffo via phone or electronic entry. She did indicate that on November 27, it was mentioned in ward rounds that your father was unhappy with his meals. As the concern seemed to be related primarily to food choices, she followed our usual practice of having our diet clerk service assist the client with marking menus and recording food preferences.

Nutrition and Food Services employs diet clerks who make daily visits to clients on the unit to help them select menu items for the following day's meals. I noticed that in the client record, the care aids at times confused the terms "diet clerk" and "dietitian". For example, on November 25 it was noted that the "dietitian in to see patient and order meals", which would likely indicate a visit by the diet clerk. It is possible that the requests to see the dietitian on November 26 and November 30 were directed erroneously to the phone number for the diet clerks instead of the dietitian and points to an opportunity to clarify communication channels with the unit staff. I sincerely apologize that your request for dietitian services went unanswered until December 4.

Although our clinical dietitians are expected to routinely screen all patients for nutritional risk, it is regrettable that the need for nutritional intervention was not identified by the unit dietitian through the screening process.

The ward dietitian has also expressed her regret that she did not identify Mr. Triffo's nutritional risk and the need for nutritional intervention earlier in his hospital stay. Your experience serves as a reminder of the importance of timely nutritional risk screening with patients and families.

I am pleased to report that the region will soon be implementing nutrition risk screening as part of the database completed by care staff upon client admission. The inclusion of nutrition risk questions upon admission will help dietitians and other care staff to identify clients, such as your father, who would benefit from early nutritional intervention during their hospital stay.

I am truly sorry that we cannot change your experience but we will endeavour to prevent such delays in service from occurring again. I thank you for bringing your concerns to my attention. The valuable feedback, from clients such as you provides us with the opportunity to improve the service that we provide.

I apologize again for failing to meet your expectations and hope that we are able to serve you and your family better in the future.

December 20, 2014

Today we decided we needed to get some rest and recuperate.

We were just getting ready to go up to the hospital after lunch when the hospital called to let Mom know that Dad is being moved to another ward. Thank goodness there was family at the hospital to help with the transfer!

The new unit is a welcome change.

There is a terrific lounge with TV's, big comfy couches, kitchen area with windows looking out to the street, microwave, dishwasher and fridge to put food in rather than having to deal with the noisy cooler we had been using.

Around the corner from his room is a beautiful family room with more big couches, a TV and a table! We got him settled in.

Elf has the perfect spot on the wall so he can "hang in there" with Dad!

When we arrived at the hospital he was sitting up in his chair visiting with company. It's been weeks since he has done that.

While he was sitting up, we tried to get him to have some soup. We had homemade and Lipton soups, but he only had a teaspoon of each.

He was tired and confused when he realized that he was still at the Pasqua Hospital. He thought he had been transferred to a Ronald McDonald House. His hallucinations were back. He was seeing fish and mice on the ceiling.

He would stare blankly at things and get upset when we didn't know what he was talking about. In the afternoon, he spent a lot of time thinking he was in a motorhome he had sold a few years prior and made a nurse walk around the ward with him to search for it.

He had spent the last three weeks in bed with no strength to move. Today, he had sat up most of the day in his chair and had a good walk. It was an impressive amount of exercise. For supper he wanted fish and fried potatoes, but then changed his mind and wanted an apple fritter and coffee.

It was a quick run to Robin's Donuts to get these for him. When he got the donut he took a HUGE bite, chewed and swallowed it while we watched in shock. It usually takes him 30 seconds to swallow a sip of water. He took two more very large bites of the donut and was also able to swallow them.

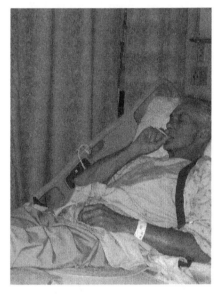

When he was done, he started searching for his cigarettes and a lighter.

To appease him, we gave him a straw to suck on. He was using it to smoke, but got very upset and said, "This cigarette is useless, take it back to where you got it from and tell them to shove it".

He proceeded to get frustrated and chucked the straw across the room.

A short while later he thought his medication was on hooks at the end of the bed.

He wants to go home, but in his confused state and needing to be on IV, combined with the stairs that he would have to get up if we took him anywhere, it's not possible.

When speaking with the nurse, we learned the confusion and hallucinations could be a side effect of the medication, but they are hoping to get the doctor to order another CT scan of his brain on Monday. We were able to calm him down enough to get him settled for the night after getting his evening medication.

The nurses on his previous ward were great, but the nurses on this ward, I'm convinced they are actually angels in scrubs.

If an IV beeps, there literally isn't enough time to stand up before a nurse is there to help.

December 21, 2014

Corie was at the hospital early this morning so I picked up Mom and took her for brunch. We were both so tired that we could barely even talk during the meal. When we got to the hospital Dad was sleeping. We were told he had pulled out his IV last night by himself. The nurses tried seven times to get another one connected, but it didn't work so he doesn't have an IV today.

The nurse had taken him for a bath earlier and he had been coherent and pleasant. When he woke up he was confused. Playing music seems to help him calm down.

Tiana started working on a puzzle in the lounge area. Mom napped in the chair by Dad's bed while I went to the family room to nap on the couch. Corie went home for the afternoon and there were a few visitors that came to visit. Dad slept some in the afternoon, but by 5 pm, Mom wasn't feeling well so I drove her back home to get some rest.

Back at the hospital, Naught E. Elf decided to change things up a little.

The note reads:

Hey Al,

I need to catch some zzz's.

Let everyone know that we are taking the day off. I am turning into grumpy elf. If Santa finds out, he will make me stay with you until next Christmas and I will miss out on 340 days of my special peppermint hot chocolate lattes with marshmallows on top.

Sweet dreams while I recharge my batteries.

Naught E. Elf

Dad got agitated again and wanted to have a cigarette. It was a feat trying to get him to understand he quit smoking and that he was in the hospital.

When he gets hungry, we have about five minutes to get him what he wants or the craving passes and he loses his appetite. At 6:30 he got hungry and we convinced him to have some stew. He wasn't pleased that it was from Robin's Donuts, he was hoping for something homemade and wanted buttered bread to go with it. Tiana ran to the lounge to get him some buttered bread. He had a spoonful of the stew and no bread before deciding he actually wanted to have KFC.

Corie was having Christmas Dinner and was on his way from across town bringing him turkey, but Dad was adamant that he wanted KFC instead.

Luckily KFC is very close to the Pasqua Hospital so I ran to get him a drumstick and fries, like he asked, and made it back to the hospital in record time. When I returned he discovered that I didn't get gravy. He was upset and disappointed with me. "Who gets KFC without gravy?" It was a valid point.

He was able to get down a bite of the drumstick and four French fries, but without the gravy, it wasn't worth eating and he went back to bed.

A few moments later Corie arrived with the homemade turkey dinner. It took bargaining to convince him to get back out of bed to try it. When he started eating, he shovelled the food down and enjoyed it. The moment he had enough, he got himself back into bed, covered up and went to sleep.

Corie and I went to the lounge to work on the puzzle leaving Taya and Tiana in the room to visit with Dad for a while. We went back to his room to get him settled for the night and the girls were able to work on the puzzle in the lounge.

The puzzles in the lounge were giving us all a much needed break. They require little thought. When you actually find a few pieces that fit, it feels like you have accomplished something. We were able to focus on something else, even if it was for a few minutes at a time.

The note reads:

Hey Trooper,

Keep hanging in there!

Naught E. Elf

The nurse came in and gave him his crushed pills in ice cream, we got him prepared for the night. We made it through another day.

Fun fact: The ice cream served in the hospital doesn't melt like normal ice cream. This is what it looked like after 30 minutes sitting on the table.

December 22, 2014

Dad had radiation again this morning.

The note reads:

Al,

Just taking a nap! Let me know when you are up and at it.

Keep warm,

Naught E. Elf

At noon Mom tried to get Dad to eat borscht, but he only had a spoonful. He slept the majority of the afternoon. They had to reconnect the IV because he is getting dehydrated.

When I got up to the hospital after work, Mom and I went to the cafeteria to get something to eat while Dad slept. The girls spent time between being staying in the hospital room with him and working on the puzzle when they needed a break.

Corie brought another turkey dinner and was able to get Dad to eat. At 8:57 pm, Dad had a craving for an oatmeal cookie. Corie and I raced to Robin's Donuts before it closed at 9 pm. The lady was just putting up the closed sign when we got to the counter, but we were able to get an oatmeal cookie, oatmeal raisin cookie and a chocolate chip cookie just in time.

When we got back to the room, we started an episode of Gold Rush on the tablet. While he was watching his show, he helped himself to the cookies, taking large bites and chewing forever. It kept all of us on the edge of our seats until we knew he was able to swallow without choking. His taste is finally coming back and so is his appetite.

The nurses have started giving him his medication with ice cream to help make them easier to swallow.

December 23, 2014

Mom got up early this morning and shovelled her sidewalk. Dad always made sure that all the snow was cleared of the driveway and she had been making sure that it was kept that way while he was in the hospital. When she finished she went in the house, poured a cup of coffee, sat down and was ready to relax. She fell asleep sitting up in her chair for a couple of hours holding her coffee instead.

Corie was at the hospital this morning when Dad went for radiation. A neighbour drove Mom up to the hospital just after lunch and a few visitors came up to the hospital to see him around 1:30 pm.

The note reads:

Hey Al,

Maybe you should try to eat a banana?

Did you know that you are actually supposed to hold them on this end to open them?

Your informant,

Naught E. Elf

Corie was having a hard time trying to wake Dad up to eat, he just wanted to sleep. I went up to the hospital to try to help with the negotiation process. It didn't work.

He is getting headaches often, so I massaged his head for a bit to try to help alleviate the pain. The girls went up to the hospital at around 4 pm to sat with Mom and Dad.

For supper tonight, he had ate three pieces of pork and a good helping of cooked carrots before going back to sleep. Mom, the girls and I went to the lounge to work on the puzzle again and have some tea. Corie came up to the hospital tonight but Dad was still sleeping so he came to work on the puzzle.

When we were tired of that, he and I went to Robin's Donuts to get something to eat. Dad had wanted a cinnamon bun so I got one while we were there and Corie got rice crispy cake. When we got back to the room, Dad was awake and ate a third of the rice crispy cake with some milk. He wanted nothing to do with the cinnamon bun and went back to sleep.

We went back to the lounge to work on the puzzle, completed it and got him ready for the night before we went home.

December 24, 2014

Mom stayed at home in the morning. Corie made it up to the hospital just after lunch and Dad sent him to get a cinnamon bun from Robin's Donuts. Rather than eating the cinnamon bun, he scraped the icing off the top and ate that instead. He also got into shortbread cookies, cherry blossom chocolates and drank a little coffee.

By the time I got to the hospital after work, Dad had decided he wanted a cigarette. He caused quite a commotion trying to find his cigarettes that didn't exist. Dad got upset with Mom and Tiana because they wouldn't get his cigarettes for him. He got himself back into bed, with his back facing them, and went to sleep frustrated.

We went to the puzzle room to find that someone had left another 500 piece puzzle on top of the puzzle we finished yesterday.

It was another project to work on.

Taya had made a beautiful Christmas tree out of fruit for Dad and took it to the hospital in an effort to get him to eat something healthier.

We managed to have him settled for the night at around 10 pm and completed the puzzle.

We went home and the girls opened their presents. It was a lovely evening with a few much needed laughs and some quiet time together.

December 25, 2014

Well, this is Christmas. We spent the morning at home resting. I was on the phone with Mom letting her know I was almost ready and would be on my way to get her when the hospital called. Dad was having an emotional day and they wanted to know when we would be coming to the hospital.

Corie went up to the hospital right away and Dad was sleeping when he arrived. I picked up Mom and we arrived at the hospital a short time later.

While talking to the nurses we learned that he was up and had a bath in the morning. A grade 5 class had made Christmas cards for the sick people in the hospital. Dad got one of those cards and it touched his heart and made him teary. The nurses comforted him and called to see when we were going to come up to the hospital a short time after that.

We set up his room to look a little more festive before the three of us went to the cafeteria. Turkey dinner was being served. While eating, we decided we would have to get him up and moving around today.

When we got back to the room, Dad was awake when we arrived. He wanted to have Costco pumpkin pie. Where do you get pumpkin pie when stores are closed on Christmas Day? It wasn't just any pumpkin pie he was asking for, he specifically wanted Costco pumpkin pie and they quit making it after Thanksgiving weekend.

Corie and I set off on mission impossible to find one. Willing to settle for any pumpkin pie, we checked a convenience store that was open close by but they didn't have any. Corie sent a text message to his friends. Thankfully, they had a frozen Costco pumpkin pie in the freezer and lived close by. JACKPOT! We picked it up and headed back to the hospital.

When we arrived in the room to tell Dad that we got his pie, he wasn't interested in it anymore. He just wanted a cherry blossom.

We went to the puzzle room and started a new puzzle while he got some rest. When we had enough of working on the puzzle and thought that he had enough rest, we decided it was time to get him moving.

We got him into a wheelchair and took him to the main level to look outside, but he was wanting a cigarette so we took him to the cafeteria for a cinnamon bun and coffee to change the scenery in hopes he would forget about smoking.

He managed to eat the majority of the cinnamon and drank half the coffee.

While sitting in the cafeteria Dad had said that eight months ago he was looking down the scope of a fishing rod and saw how this journey ended. He told us he has between three weeks to a month. When we asked when that would be, he said before the end of January. His hallucinations were a mix of reality and something in his mind, but this one took us back. It was something none of us wanted to hear.

We took him to the lounge when he was done in the cafeteria. We sat in there for a while as he ate three devilled eggs and looked around. He got tired and wanted to go back to bed.

It wasn't long before he started having another cigarette episode. This time he became very agitated was determined to get what he wanted. He got into a wheelchair and was headed to the nearest exit with the rest of us following close behind. He knew exactly where he was and how to get out. Instead of going to the cafeteria like he wanted, I had pushed level one in the elevator, hoping to distract him. That was a bad idea. He let me know exactly what he thought in no uncertain terms as we wheeled him out of one elevator directly into another that took us to the basement like he initially wanted.

He demanded to go outside to have a cigarette. We managed to find a jacket to cover him up and keep him warm before leaving the building. It was a month and a half that he went without a cigarette and he finished one with no problem. When Corie brought him back inside Dad had a grin from ear to ear. He was happy as can be.

When we got him back upstairs his meal was ready. It was a real turkey dinner that he could enjoy.

We took him to the lounge and he ate most of it.

For our family Christmas Dinner we went to the cafeteria to get ham and scalloped potato meals for everyone else. We were able to eat together as a family in the lounge and it was wonderful.

Dad opened his gift and decided he wanted to go to bed.

When Corie was wheeling him back to his room, Dad was confused as to where his bed went. He had thought he was going home.

When we got him settled into bed, the rest of us went to my house to open gifts, then over to Corie's to watch a movie. Mom had stayed at our house and we had an early night.

It was a bittersweet Christmas. We had Dad with us, for that we were grateful.

December 26, 2014

Today I am very tired. We got up and I drove Mom home to change her clothes before going to the hospital. Dad was sleeping when we got into his room.

I stuffed elf into a drink container to add a little humor to the room.

The note read:

HELP!

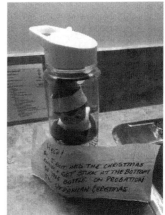

Al, I got into the Christmas cheer and got stuck at the bottom of the bottle.

On probation until Ukrainian Christmas.

Naught E. Elf

I checked with the nurse and she said he was sleeping for most of the morning, but had got up two times in the night to go to the bathroom. He didn't eat breakfast or lunch. We sat with him for a while before Mom and I went to eat in the cafeteria.

Mom stayed with him while I went to work and she spent the afternoon emptying a plastic urinal eight times. Something was different, that never happened before, but no one knew what it could be.

He ate a piece of lemon meringue pie, a few peas and potatoes before going back to sleep. When I arrived at 6:30 pm he was still sleeping.

His face and neck were flushed but he felt really cold. His heart rate had slowed. The heart specialist was called in to look at him and Dad was taken off his heart medications.

His ankles aren't swelling but his face looked puffy and the back of his head still hurts.

He was cranky and tired. Mom and I spent some time in the puzzle room and waited to make sure he was settled before we left the hospital.

December 27, 2014

Went to pick up Mom to take her to the hospital before heading for lunch with a friend. Spent a good portion of the afternoon having a good chat over potato soup and tea at the 13th Avenue Coffee House. It was a wonderful way to lift my spirits before going back up to the hospital to visit Dad.

When I got there he was awake, but very tired and wanted to sleep. I went to the puzzle room to set up todays puzzle and talked to a few other families.

Taya came in and helped sort the puzzle pieces by colour and edges into little Styrofoam plates to help the 1000 piece puzzle be a little easier to put together.

We had left the puzzle once the pieces were sorted and went to the cafeteria to get some food.

When we came back, Dad was awake so we got to visit with him for a bit. One of his visitors asked him when he was going home. In his confused state, that thought got stuck in his mind. We spent the majority of the day trying to keep him comfortable in the hospital while the doctors worked to get him stabilized.

He wasn't feeling well today, his stomach hurt, his head hurt when he ate and food is starting to taste funny again to him. He was having problems breathing so I rubbed his back and held onto his arm until he calmed down.

A few moments after we finally got him to sleep, the nurse came in to give him his pills. It took a while to get him settled again and sleeping. He was hot, then cold, then his stomach hurt, then he was confused. Eventually he turned onto his side. By lightly holding his arm he became less agitated and fell asleep.

December 28, 2014

Today we were at the hospital at noon. Dad was awake when he got there staring at his dinner plate. He had chocolate milk, beef stew with potatoes, green beans, cranberry juice, ice cream, chicken soup and some strawberries.

As he sat on the edge of the bed hunched over his table, it was obvious the smell of the food was making his stomach turn.

He was hungry but couldn't eat because his taste is off. He gags on anything that doesn't have the right texture or certain flavors. He ate his strawberries, and I took the stew off his table so he didn't have to smell it before going to the cafeteria to get a Denver sandwich, chicken fingers with fries, cottage cheese, lemon pudding, and pumpkin pie in a desperate effort to try to find something, anything, that he could eat. When I got back, I set up everything on his tray and let him pick and choose what he wanted to eat.

He ate all of the pumpkin pie, tried to eat some egg out of the Denver but had to spit it out, drank all of his chocolate milk, had a few teaspoons of cottage cheese, a few teaspoons of the lemon pudding, a few bites of chicken fingers and a couple fries. He tried to eat some of the potatoes and beans too. Lunch was a success, kind of. It's more junk food than we want to see him eat, but it's better than him starving at this point.

He has been adamant that he wants goody rings, but we had taken them home yesterday.

When Corie came, he bought him a bounty bar and Dad ate both pieces of it. His blood sugars were 14.7. Then he got into the chocolates, ate fudge and rosebuds. He was alert and awake, but very frustrated with the hospital food. The smell literally makes him sick and turns his stomach. I can't say I blame him because it usually turns mine too.

They have tried to give him better food since the dietician was in, but it isn't working. The frustration brought him to tears today and I let him know that it was his job to rest and heal while we fought the battle for him.

We were able to calm him and he got some rest. He wasn't hungry at supper time. We got him settled into bed early tonight and came home.

December 29, 2014

Mom and I got up to the hospital just before noon today and Dad was hooked up to a heart monitor and trying to sleep. He told us he ate a pancake and some cream of wheat for breakfast. We went for lunch and he was still sleeping when we got back to the room so I went back to work.

Dad had got up and ate a good lunch, had a visit with company and was awake when I got to the hospital at 7:30 pm. He ate some cabbage rolls today. He also got into his bag of treats that were in his closet to find a cherry blossom chocolate which tells me he has to be feeling better. We got some smiles out of him when we started teasing him. He looks good and wanted a coffee so I went to Robins get it and got an oatmeal cookie too.

Tiana stayed with him until he fell asleep and we went to the puzzle room for a while before coming home.

December 30, 2014

Today Dad was tired and had slept for most of the day. Tonight he did eat some of this supper, but we couldn't convince him to eat the cabbage rolls that were brought for him.

The doctor talked to Mom in the family room. The goal is to try to get him to eat and drink on his own so that he can be taken off the IV. They are hoping that he can go home for a couple hours next weekend.

December 31, 2014

Today we are all exhausted. Corie was at the hospital by noon and Dad was up eating lunch, sitting on the edge of the bed and able to walk. He is a bit wobbly but the physical therapists are getting him moving.

Taya drove Mom to the hospital mid-afternoon. I was at the hospital after work when Dad got his supper. He was able to eat the pork today. I went to the lounge because I was played out and needed rest.

We had company visit at the hospital and they brought everything needed to celebrate New Year's Eve. Cheese, crackers, pop, chocolates, veggies, dip and even a little cheer. Dad had fun and enjoyed the party.

I couldn't reach Taya so I went home to find her sleeping on the couch so tired that she wasn't able to hear the phone. Tiana went to a friends for the night. I went back to the hospital and got to visit.

One of the ladies we met while Dad was on the unit got to go home today. She will go to Saskatoon January 12th for three months for treatment. We said goodbye to her and her family.

We worked on the puzzle for a bit while we waited to make sure Dad was settled.

January 1, 2015

Today we got to sleep. When we got to the hospital Dad was sitting up and unable to eat the hospital food that they brought him.

It was ribs and potatoes, but the smell turned his stomach. We brought oatmeal up to the hospital and were able to get a little bit into him today with his whole milk. Dad went back to sleep once he finished the small bowl of oatmeal while Mom and I went to the cafeteria to have turkey dinner.

We had a quick visit with Dad's roommate. She is in the middle of having her 96 hour chemo treatment and is very positive. It's so good to see.

Dad was visiting with Mom and Taya while I went to the lounge to get another puzzle ready for the families and to make sure Dad's room wasn't crowded. Today one of the other patients decided to quit taking treatments because it is too much for him. It's been a sad day for that family as they are faced to coming to terms with letting go.

Everyone comes in to help or check on the puzzle to see how it is coming along. Mom came into the lounge when Dad was sleeping. Taya started one of her drawings for school.

When we went to check on Dad, he decided he was going to get up and go for a walk today. This was exciting news! What a great way to start the New Year! Dad was wobbly, so we got him a wheelchair. He was able to sit up for an hour and a half in the lounge! I made him tea and he was able to have a few sips, but it started tasting funny and he couldn't have any more.

His meal came at 5 pm and we brought the tray into the lounge. It was turkey dinner. He ate most of it and even wanted more, but he was tired.

He asked how many times he had been home since he got to the hospital. We let him know that he hadn't been out of the hospital yet. He replied, "I thought I've been home a hundred times already, I go home all the time". Although he had confused moments, he was aware of what was going on for the most part. Doctors are uncertain of what is causing the confusion.

I'm hoping it goes away as he is able to eat more food. His sweet tooth definitely isn't malfunctioning. His blood sugars are at 19. We are going to focus on getting more protein into him and less sugar if we can. It's so hard when we have to rely on his craving at the moment to determine what he will eat.

We got him back to his room and settled before heading down to the cafeteria to eat another turkey dinner for supper. Mom got Dad more turkey meat and mashed potatoes with gravy hoping he would eat some more. He said he felt really full and didn't want to eat in case he threw everything up.

We put his meal in the fridge. For lunch tomorrow he can have turkey, mashed potatoes and cabbage rolls.

Dad got company tonight and enjoyed his visit. We worked on the puzzle a little more and were able to visit with a different couple that the wife has had cancer a few times. She is now battling liver and lung cancer.

We went home early tonight because we are all tired. Mom came home with us because she had to go up to the hospital early and I had work in the morning.

So far 2015 is good.

January 2, 2015

We went to the hospital to get Dad ready for his haircut.

The doctor told him that he could go home from 10 am until 8 pm tomorrow. Dad's meal was sitting on his table. The doctor lifted the cover to see how much he had eaten. Under the lid, she found a plate with a scoop of scrambled eggs and a slice of toast, untouched. She asked him if he was going to eat any of it. He asked her if she would eat it. I guess she had said no because Dad's response was, "Well I won't eat it either". He did manage to eat some cream of wheat.

We got Dad into the wheelchair and took him for his haircut. He looks great! We wheeled him around the halls to view the scenery before taking him to the cafeteria to try to find him something to eat.

The menu was battered fish and a chicken wrap which didn't interest him. They also had mushroom soup. We got a small container for him to try, but it didn't taste right and we had to get him out of the cafeteria area because his senses made him think that everything was burnt.

We went to the first floor to try Robins Donuts. He spotted a butter tart and wanted two of them with chocolate milk. He was able to have a few sips of milk and a half of tart before they had to go back to his room.

In the afternoon, Mom took him to the lobby and they sat in there for a long time. He just got settled back into bed when I came up to the hospital with Safeway fried chicken, Kentucky Fried Chicken, KFC fries with gravy, a fruit tray, popcorn twists, chips and dip. I also heated up his turkey and cabbage rolls to give him lots of options to eat. The smell took over the whole ward but he was able to eat a little of the turkey, cabbage rolls and a few fries with gravy. When he was done eating, we took him back to his room to get settled and let him sleep.

It was 6:19 pm when we left the hospital today. That's the soonest we have ever left, but we needed to go to a grocery store and it had been snowing all day. After we got groceries, I took Mom home and shoveled her driveway while saying a prayer that it will be done snowing for the week.

January 3, 2015

I woke up to the phone ringing. It was Mom letting me know that Dad was being released from the hospital at 10 am. My vehicle was the easiest for him to get in and out of and I could pick her up on the way to the hospital.

We walked into his room ten minutes early expecting him to be up and ready to go, but found him sprawled out in bed with his ankles crossed staring at the clock. When we asked him what he was doing, he said, "I'm just laying here". While Mom helped him get dressed, I went to the lounge to work on the puzzle and make sure the vehicle was started because it is -22 today.

The nurse got all his medications ready for us to take for the day. When I went back into the room, he looked like he was swimming in his shirt and pants. We got him into the wheelchair and headed for the exit. We met Corie going around the corner and I ran to the parking lot to get the

vehicle. Dad was not impressed with the cold weather. We got him into the house and in his chair where he usually sat, he ate some raisin toast with peanut butter, a cup of chocolate milk and some butterscotch pudding. The heartburn was back as soon as he finished eating.

Dad was adamant that there was Divol in the cupboard on the top shelf in the bathroom, but there wasn't any there. A quick trip to the grocery store was required.

By 11:15 am, he was ready for a nap. While walking to his bedroom, his jeans literally fell to his knees, belt included. Mom got him settled for his nap and Corie started on the mission to find him some smaller jeans to wear. Dad was freezing, so a few flannel blankets were heated in the dryer to help get him warmed up.

There was a new house being built in the lot beside them and he got to watch from his bedroom window as it was being worked on.

He wanted hamburgers for supper and gave exact instructions on how to make them. I was to make them at my house so the smell of the burgers cooking wouldn't bother him. Before I could get out of the house, he mentioned that he may want harvest sausages and harvest thick bacon (not the thin stuff). He also decided that he was going to fry an egg with a little butter when he got up. He thought he would be able to eat that.

I had an appointment today at 1:30 pm, so I got everything needed from Safeway and took it back to Mom and Dad's before the meeting. I had brought back some Harvest ham sausage and he decided he wanted a thin piece of it. He was able to take a large bite but had to put it away because something wasn't right. Then he got to go to his own bed to have a sleep.

That evening, he needed to be back at the hospital, but Dad thought it would be a better idea to spend the night at home. It took Mom and Corie a while to get him dressed, because he wasn't interested in helping them get him ready to leave. We managed to get him to the hospital and settled before 9 pm.

<u>Family Update January 3rd</u>

We expected to go to the hospital at 10 am and see Dad sitting on the edge of the bed waiting to go home, but that was not the case. He was sprawled out in his hospital gear completely relaxed. We got him up and dressed but he is swimming in his clothes.

At 146 lbs he literally walked out of his pants when we got him home, but he did amazing! He ate more than he has in three weeks. He was able to spend time sitting up and got a good sleep in his own bed.

He is back at the hospital for tomorrow, but we are hoping to bring him home Monday night. It was an amazing day! All is well.

This is Dad all bundled up and ready to fly back to the hospital. He still has his sense of humor!

January 4, 2015

Dad was up and energetic today but is frustrated with the health care system. Just the smell of the hospital food is enough to turn his stomach. He doesn't understand why patients just can't get their food from the cafeteria if it is better than the hospital food. Why do patients have to pay for edible food if the hospital can't supply it in the room?

When he went to visit his old nurses he got into a conversation with them about being asked everyday if he was ready to go home. People are discharged and sometimes have to be brought back by ambulance because they weren't ready to leave in the first place.

Why are millions of dollars being spent on Mosaic Stadium while our sickest citizens are being served disgraceful meals in hospitals with not enough beds? He is determined to get better so that his story can be told and his point heard.

Family Update January 4th

We got to the hospital in time for lunch. Hospital food wasn't an option for him today so we went and got him chicken noodle soup from Robins.

He ate all four of the muffins that were made by a family friend and he let it be known that the dietary staff needs to take lessons from her on how to cook because he can eat those with no problem. He also had ice cream, apple juice, fruit, chocolate milk and two slices of raisin toast with peanut butter.

We thought he would have been played out so the plan was to let him sleep. I went to the puzzle room for ten minutes. He came walking in and sat down beside the window for a while. When he got tired, we put him in a wheelchair to take him back to the room. He decided he wanted to go on a hospital tour instead. We took him to visit his nurses on the old ward, before going to Shoppers, Robins Donuts and the cafeteria where he got chocolate milk and two pieces of fish. He ate it all!

We got him back to his room and were sure that he was going to need a nap. I went back to the puzzle room to let him get some rest, but a few minutes later he wheeled in and checked out every cupboard in the kitchen.

When he got tired we took him back to his room, but he decided he was going for a hot bath before bed. He sat and enjoyed the tub for 15 minutes tonight and was in bed resting by 7:30 pm!

This has been the biggest day he has had since November 13th and we could not be more proud of him! We are hoping he will have enough strength to come back home by the end of the week.

January 5, 2015

Dad had a good night, he slept and wasn't overly interested in the breakfast that they brought him. He did eat some cream of wheat.

At lunch time they brought macaroni and cheese with peas. When we lifted the lid, the smell bothered him so we took it out of his room. I ran down to Mia Fresco and got him some chicken soup with brown rice, celery, green onion and carrots and a hot chocolate that he had asked for. He ate a small bowl of the soup and drank his hot chocolate before I left to go to go back to work. Corie brought up some muffins and coffee cake that a friend had made for him and he was so excited! He said more than once it isn't impossible to find something that people in his condition can eat.

He was able to walk around the ward a few times today with a physiotherapist. His walking is improving. In the afternoon he got up and went to the TV room and watched a movie.

The doctor told him the goal is to be able to let Dad go home on Thursday.

For supper he was served perogies, ham and carrots. Again, we lifted the lid and the smell turned his stomach. We got rid of the tray. He ate canned pears, a bite of pizza from the cafeteria, chocolate milk, coffee cake and tried whole milk, but it was warm. He gave up on eating and decided he was going to sleep.

His upbeat neighbor left today. The new neighbour is facing end of life and her family is having a hard time coming to terms with letting her go. They opted for taking all measures to keep her alive as long as possible. The patient is connected to oxygen and a feeding tube. There is a doctor or nurse working on her most of the day. The sounds are hard to listen to and it is hard to stay positive when being surrounded with so much sadness and distress. I'm hoping the days go fast so we can get him out of here sooner than later.

January 6, 2015

Dad had a good sleep last night. The doctor came in today and they are going to be working with palliative care to send him home. They will be able to provide everything we need. A home care nurse will be making regular visits and will also take care of his medications for him as well.

The doctor told him when his medications were adjusted in the past few weeks, his heart rate had dropped to 30 beats per minute. That has been worked out and may explain some of the confusion he had been experiencing. Due to his tremendous weight loss, some medications are no longer required. That is good news!

He was up for the majority of the day and sat in the lounge. Dad went to the cafeteria and ate some Italian wedding soup, came back upstairs and had more soup. He was able to eat his shepherd's pie for supper tonight, a muffin, coffee cake and started drinking G2 drinks.

He told us that he will be eating and getting his weight back within a month. His spirits are better than I've seen them in a very long time. It is obvious he is excited to come home. He has heartburn and is weak but he can walk with a walker and sit up in a wheelchair for a few hours a day.

Taya had a basketball game tonight that Tiana, Mom and I were able to go watch. It gave us a change of scenery. It will be great when Dad can get out to watch another game.

January 7, 2015

Today when we got to the hospital we were informed that the plan was to discharge him today. The nurses were running around getting all the discharge papers and requisition forms for Saskatchewan Abilities Council so we can get a walker, bathtub chair, etc. on loan, as well as a list of the medications that he will be taking once he leaves the hospital.

Mom and I went to the cafeteria and met up with Corie for lunch. Mom left to go to Dad's room first. When Corie and I got to his room, the bed was empty. We went to the lounge to discover Dad had walked to the lounge by himself.

We were sitting in there for a while waiting for necessary Saskatchewan Abilities paperwork to get the equipment required to take him home. Dad got dizzy sitting in the chair so he went back to his bed to sleep.

He liked the Powerade drinks but the doctor recommended Gatorade instead because the salt content should help increase his blood pressure. He is getting a bit stronger, his digestive system seems to be working better, the headache is subsiding, but his heartburn is still bad. His neck and shoulder are starting to hurt again.

The doctor came into see him. She said his vitals and blood work are good so he is ready to go home. We told her that he is dizzy and she is wanting to watch him for a while. A short while later we learned that he was going to have to wait until tomorrow to go home. He got company so Corie and I went to work for the rest of the afternoon while Mom stayed with him.

When I got back to the hospital after work Dad was sleeping. He had been feeling dizzy and sick. We had an appointment booked with a foot care nurse, but she was sick and had to cancel. We got him set up for the night before I took Mom home.

Tomorrow is another day.

January 8, 2015

Today I was at work early then went to pick up Mom mid-morning. The hospital called just before I arrived to let Mom know Dad is up, had a bath, ready and waiting to go home. It was a very cold day today with wind.

When we got to his hospital room Dad was sprawled out in the bed with his hospital gear on looking uninterested and unenergetic. Mom was getting him up to get dressed so I went to the puzzle room to work on the puzzle until she was finished. We got everything packed up and headed for the exit! It was 59 consecutive days in the hospital and we were so excited to get him home.

Once we got him into the house, we sat him on his regular chair at the table before Mom and I went out to do errands. We had to get his medication and go to Sask Abilities Council to pick up a walker and a bath chair. On our way home we stopped to pick up a pill sorter and some smaller sweats that would fit him. He just got up from a nap when we returned.

He ate some borscht, harvest ham sausage and drank vitamin water before getting tired and going to back to lay down again. When he was settled in his bed, I opened the blinds in their bedroom window so he could see outside. Mom was sorting his pills while I talked to him.

It was time for me to go back to work and I was putting on my shoes when he started yelling from the bedroom. I went back to his room to see what he wanted and he told me the power was out. His room was dark, but the TV was on and the air filter was still running. The power couldn't be off. I turned on the light, but the room was still darker than it had been before. I thought maybe the sun just went behind the clouds but when I looked the blinds between the window panes had been closed completely. Dad and I were the only two that had been in the room in those few moments and neither of us closed the blinds. I opened them again to let him look out the window before going back to the office.

He slept for a while but didn't eat supper tonight. Mom looks tired today. The girls and I will go over to help tomorrow night.

Family Update January 8th

Dad has been discharged from the hospital and is resting at home.

January 9, 2015

Dad ate at lunch today but was not hungry at supper and is not interested in talking about food.

He is able to stay up longer throughout the day and is working hard at his exercises where he stands up and sits down on a chair. He is hoping to be able to walk down stairs soon so he can have a shower rather than going having to go into the bathtub upstairs. He weighed himself today and he is 142 lbs with his layered clothes on.

Taya and I are spending the night there tonight to help out if it is needed.

January 10, 2015

It was an uneventful night! Dad only had to go to the bathroom once and slept through the night waking up at 8:30 am. That is a huge improvement. He used to get up six times a night on a regular basis for years.

With the weather being so cold, Dad was concerned about his van not being able to start. Corie said he could go over with the charger to get the vehicle started, but Dad was still pondering over it.

When he got up, Taya made him some scrambled eggs, but he wasn't crazy about them. He said they tasted funny. He tried a little coffee but it taste bitter to him. We got him to eat a muffin so Taya decided that she was going to bake for him.

She started out with baking the muffins but Dad couldn't see what she was doing from the kitchen chair so we got his wheelchair and put it in the kitchen. That helped him get more mobile so he could help with the process. Mom had to get some groceries and there were extra items needed for the baking. I took Mom shopping while Taya stayed home with Dad to bake.

We went to Safeway to get the canned fruit cocktail that Dad had requested and some of the baking supplies, then we headed over to the wholesaler to get some more items. It was exciting to be able to do activities outside of the hospital. I got a few calls to add more items to the list because Taya and Dad decided to make matrimonial cake. Dad is wanting company to visit. A few boxes of Tim Horton's Timbits to serve were requested just in case someone decides to come by.

I dropped Mom off at home before going to pick up Tiana from her sleepover. We had to go to the Cornwall to pick up a few things and stopped by Zam Zam to get Taya a vegan supper. With all the baking that she is doing, I was sure she was going to need a feast for herself because she couldn't eat anything she had baked.

When Tiana and I went back to Mom and Dad's, the house smelled like a bakery. They baked peach muffins, bran muffins, cinnamon buns, buns, Saskatoon pie, Saskatoon tarts and matrimonial cake. Thank goodness it all tasted good to him so he could eat and enjoy it. Dad ate the baking for supper, some sausage, a couple G2, but wanted chocolate milk with the saskatoon pie.

Dad called Corie to see if he could bring chocolate milk on his way over to get the van started. Corie had planned on getting the van started tomorrow but agreed to come over and pick up some chocolate milk on his way.

We were all sitting around talking for a half hour, but the wait was getting to be too long for him, so I headed to Safeway to get the chocolate milk. I made it all the way to the back of the grocery store when the phone rang. Corie was at the house with the chocolate milk, so Dad didn't need anymore. I left and headed back to their house to find the van started.

Dad was much more content, but was wanting a cigarette. Corie gave him an electronic one to try to help him forget about it, but that didn't work.

Dad tested his blood sugars and they were 7.6 tonight. His blood pressure was 102 over 50. Taya decided to spend another night at grandma and grandpa's house. Tiana wanted a friend to come over so we left to pick up her friend and drop them off at home before I headed back to help get Dad settled.

Mom's stomach wasn't feeling well and she wanted to go to sleep. Dad was staying up to watch the newest episode of Gold Rush and the news. It was 10:30 pm before he was ready for bed today. He is much better and was up most of the day concentrated on building strength by doing his exercises. It was a very good day. We are grateful he is getting stronger and his appetite is increasing.

January 11, 2015

Taya came home around noon today and let us know that grandpa slept through the night and slept in until 10:30 am. He wasn't hungry for breakfast. She made him a blueberry smoothie. He drank it but he wasn't thrilled about it. Mom called shortly after Taya got home to let us know that Dad had eaten three eggs and a couple buns for lunch. They tasted normal. That was exciting news.

Dad weighed himself today. With his clothes on he is 143 lbs. At least he is starting to gain a little weight rather than lose more. He is getting frustrated with the slow recovery process.

To have a bath, Corie goes over to their house to help Mom get Dad in and out of the tub because the stairs are still too much to manage for him to go downstairs to have a shower.

This afternoon Dad really wanted a cigarette. He was going to walk to the store because Mom wouldn't go for him. He stood outside on the enclosed deck for a while before coming back inside. He had three cigarettes left when he collapsed on November 14th that were still in his coat pocket. Mom gave him one and he went into the computer room with his wheelchair and had three puffs before putting it out. Thank goodness it didn't taste great to him, but he is still having cravings. He says that smoking relaxes him.

Dad had some stew. He was eating saskatoon pie and ice cream when Tiana and I arrived. He continued to eat some matrimonial cake and fruit cocktail. He had ran out of chocolate milk and was having severe cravings, again. He decided he wanted the 7 mg Nicoderm patches like he had in the hospital to try to offset them. He wants to quit smoking, but doesn't want to suffer like he has been for the past two months. It is completely understandable after smoking for 56 years. I had to get groceries anyway, so I left Tiana at Mom and Dad's to visit while I headed back to Safeway to do some shopping which included a four litre jug of chocolate milk and two 7 mg packages of Nicoderm.

Those packages sat in their kitchen cupboard and never did get opened.

Dad sat on his chair and enjoyed eating his food. We sliced up the rest of the matrimonial cake and put it into bags to be frozen. He investigated his medications and cut his fingernails while Tiana, Mom and I worked on a puzzle. We had a good afternoon visiting.

He is wanting to walk up and down the stairs and is hoping to try them soon. He is thinking he can go up and down on his bum but he would have to build up his arm strength first. There are a lot of steps and he has observed there is little padding on his backside. Even with sitting on pillows in his chair his butt gets sore. He has decided being skinny is overrated, especially because he is cold all the time. He is wanting an electric blanket. It will be tomorrow's task to find one.

Tonight Dad had said that he would like to hop into the van and drive to the Atlantic Ocean, jump in and then drive back to Vancouver. It sounds like a great idea, but he thinks he would get tired out. I suggested maybe we could go to Watrous instead and go swimming for the day. He seems to like that idea, but we will have to see how the days go.

Dad tested his blood sugars tonight and they were 13.3. He got tired at around 9 pm. We got him settled into bed before coming home to rest for the night.

Mom is getting tired and is aching all over. She thinks she just needs to rest.

January 12, 2015

Today Dad woke up at 9:30 am. He had two eggs and two pieces of toast for breakfast. Wanting to go downstairs for a shower, he tried to walk down the four back steps. He needs more time to build up his strength but did manage those stairs twice today. That is amazing!

The nurse came by today and she was impressed with his progress. Dad is having a hard time not smoking. The nurse said if he wants to smoke, let him smoke because he is under enough stress. He did have a few puffs of a cigarette today and has a plan, but none of us know what it is.

He ate some cream of wheat tonight and said that it was the best meal that he has had yet. There was some bacon but it still isn't tasting right to him.

Tiana and Dad had got out the Risky Business game that they have been playing for a year and "the bank" finally went broke today. They adjusted the rules so they just take money from each other. The game could go on forever at that rate.

He laid down after supper and spent some time visiting. The topic of going to Watrous Mineral Spa came up. It would be great for him to float in that water, but it is a two hour drive and there isn't a hospital there. For an adventure closer to home, we decided going to the Moose Jaw Temple Gardens to try that pool first.

He doesn't want to plan anything in advance just in case he isn't feeling good on that day, but we are hoping that we can go one day next week. It is something that we can all look forward too, but he will need a much smaller pair of swim trunks.

Corie came over tonight and helped Dad in and out of the bathtub so he was able to enjoy a 20 minute soak. He had a very good day today and stayed up until almost 11:30 pm.

That is the longest day he has had in a very long time.

January 13, 2015

Dad got up early today and was able to eat a bran muffin. He was tired, but he had a big day yesterday. Today will be a relaxing day for him. Tiana was trying to teach Dad how to work a program on the computer. They were very concentrated on the process.

Dad ate around 4 pm so he wasn't very hungry for supper. He had another cigarette today. His blood sugars were at 5 this morning, his digestive system is starting to work better without having to take medication to keep things moving and when he weighed himself today, without his sweater on, he was 142 lbs.

I went back to Mom and Dad's to visit for a bit and took Dad his pickled roll mops. He was up watching an episode of Gold Rush and had another long day.

January 14, 2015

Dad had a nap in the afternoon, but was up for most of the day.

Corie went to Mom and Dad's today to get the battery replaced in the van because it froze again. He ran into difficulty and wasn't able to get it to work.

I stopped at Mom and Dad's for a bit before heading going out to a movie. When I opened the patio door cigarette smoke filled the air. I asked Dad how many cigarettes he had. He claimed one, but I never bought that story. After the show, I went back to their house. The patio smelled like he just finished another cigarette. He told me the outcome would be the same whether he smoked or didn't. It's his body and his choice.

January 16, 2015

Corie went to Mom and Dad's today and got the battery fixed in their van. Dad is happy. He managed to walk downstairs by himself to check on the homemade sour cabbage that he is making.

He sent Mom to the store for a few things. When she was gone, he got on his coat and took off outside into the back alley to watch the neighbour work on building the house. On the way back home, Mom got him inside and he laid down to rest.

He was looking out the window and got excited when he saw his friend that lived beside the neighbour. He got back up, put on his coat and raced out to talk to him. Dad was coming back onto their deck when he collapsed. Luckily Corie was there to catch him and help him back onto the deck where he sat and had a good visit with his friend and Corie.

Taya stopped in to visit after school.

January 17, 2015

Tiana and I went over to Mom and Dads to visit. He is starting to get more energy, just not fast enough for his liking.

January 19, 2015

Dad stayed at home by himself while I ran Mom out for errands. He is continuing to improve every day, but he is smoking more and more too.

January 23, 2015

Dad is feeling better. Mom drove to the casino last night and they stayed out until 4 am. Dad won $2,000 and is very happy.

January 24, 2015

Dad was very tired after his late night adventure and big win last night.

January 25, 2015

Mom and Dad came over to watch a movie. We got the show started before I took Tiana out with me to get groceries for tomorrow.

January 26, 2015

Mom and Dad came by to watch a show at my place with the girls. The girls were busy doing homework and were delayed starting the movie. Mom and Dad went next door to watch a show at Corie's house instead. They stayed out until 1 am. It is amazing to see them getting in some fun days.

January 27, 2015

Tonight when I went over to Mom and Dad's. Dad had noticed that there was a lump developing on his neck. He said it was the size of a pimple the other day and now it is about the size a pea.

He has a doctor's appointment tomorrow morning so he can get it checked. He is able to walk downstairs and is more mobile. This afternoon they were at a grocery store and he walked up and down every aisle. It is unbelievable how much he has improved from a month ago.

January 28, 2015

This morning Dad went to the doctor and let him know that the food in a concentration camp had to be better than the food that they were serving in the hospital.

When the physician looked at the lumps on Dad's neck he said that they were just cysts and told him with the treatments Dad is taking that life expectancy is significant.

The news must've put Dad in really good spirits because they headed back to Casino Regina and stayed out until 3:30 am. This time he came home with $400 and had a lot of fun.

January 29, 2015

Last night's adventure wore Dad out. He slept until 6 pm and was back in bed by 9:30 pm for the night. All this partying is catching up to him.

January 30, 2015

Today Dad had an appointment with his new medical oncologist. We all met at the Allan Blair clinic at 9 am. When the nurse took Dad to weigh him, he weighed 159 lbs. We gasped in shock. That was the best news any of us could hope to hear that morning!

His new oncologist is amazing, he has great bedside manner and great stories that put everyone at ease. When he looked at the bumps on Dad's neck he wasn't convinced they were cysts, so he has ordered procedures for a biopsy to be done. A new lump started to grow at the front of his throat and he has one in his armpit now too.

The doctor explained that if it is indeed the cancer spreading that Dad's cancer will not respond to the alternative to chemo pill. The chemo that he would take would be one with the least amount of side effects. He can expect to lose some hair and experience some nausea, but treatments would be every three weeks. He also explained that the radiation wouldn't work if it is spreading because the tumor would have to be in one spot. Chemotherapy goes throughout the body, so it would be the option for treatment. Although it won't kill the cancer completely, there is a chance it could put it into remission. The appointment for chemo is being booked in the event that the growths are cancerous to prevent delays in trying to get chemo booked. We went on a tour of the chemotherapy section of the clinic and will go back to meet with the doctor in three to four weeks.

The home care nurse was out to see Dad today. They were able to order the Ensure and Boost under the palliative care program.

The nurse told Dad that he is the best patient she has right now. Mom and Dad had to take forms to Dad's family doctor to get filled out today and then decided to hit the Casino for supper. They stayed there for a few hours, but came home earlier tonight.

Feb 7, 2015

We went out for supper to Uplands Pizza to celebrate a birthday. Dad tried to eat, but he is losing his appetite again. Worried about the growing lumps, we are waiting for his appointment with the oncologist to see if there is anything that can be done.

February 27, 2015

Had the meeting with the medical oncologist this morning. Bad news. The biopsy came back and his lumps are malignant. Chemo for the type of cancer Dad has is not recommended.

If he chooses to take chemo, there is a 30 percent chance that it will help with a very good chance that he will be sick.

The doctor thought he had about a month with no treatment, potentially four months with treatment. Dad opted for treatment and starts chemo on Monday.

March 1, 2015

Dad hasn't been feeling good and is tired all the time. He is unable to eat much other than Ensure or Boost.

The lumps are growing. His energy levels are low and he is walking slower than he has been for a while. For the past month he has been weepy again.

Worry is getting the best of him.

March 2, 2015

This morning we were at the hospital early for his first chemo treatment. It took five hours.

He felt good during the treatment, had more energy than he has had in a while, looked good and is in better spirits. He said he didn't feel sick and joked about wanting to go to the casino.

We picked up his medication before taking him home.

March 3, 2015

Dad had his appointment with the radiology oncologist today. He was still feeling good but said he woke up in a sweat in the middle of the night and was drenched. After talking things through, it is thought that he may have been given some acetaminophen, because that happens to him when he takes it.

The radiologist had been on vacation and hadn't seen him since he was lying in his hospital bed, hallucinating and unable to eat or walk. There was a drastic change and she was amazed by his improvements. With the previous symptoms he was experiencing before Christmas, she wasn't expecting that his body would have improved enough to allow him to make it out of the hospital.

We found out that the tumor did shrink and that the spot in his brain is small, but it could be treated with radiation providing that the chemo helps shrink the lumps. The procedure would have to be done in Winnipeg. She is going to see him during his next chemo treatment to see how he is feeling. It was a good appointment and some hope returned to the situation.

He felt good until he got home and then his stomach got queasy. Gravol took away the sick feeling so far but he is more tired tonight.

He was put on a steroid and his blood sugars are increasing.

March 4, 2015

Dad was rushed to the hospital by ambulance because he got chest pains and severe pain in his legs. It took a while for them to control the pain in emergency.

Just before midnight he was admitted to 3B to try to get the pain under control. Being admitted to the hospital this time, he is still in better shape than he was when he was discharged last time.

His hospital bed is beside a window which helps because he can look out to see the great outdoors and watch the weather improve.

March 5, 2015

Today we took Dad on a tour of the hospital so he could figure out the building. The last time he was in the hospital he was hallucinating so it didn't make sense to him.

He is up and around more, the pain is starting to subside, but it is definitely not managed yet.

His lumps have started to shrink and he is happy about that.

March 10, 2015

Dad is finally feeling better and his pain is managed.

He woke up with his arm four times its normal size today because the IV leaked throughout the night. It took four nurses seven tries to get another IV started in his other arm. Dad isn't a fan of needles to begin with, so he wasn't very happy.

He is feeling better and we are hoping that he can come home tomorrow.

March 11, 2015

We got to take Dad home at supper time today and he is feeling good. It is good to have him back in his surroundings so he can have some uninterrupted sleep in his own bed.

For the next few weeks, Dad was feeling well, able to sleep and could eat his Ensure, Boost, eggs and toast. He ventured around town a little but left the driving to Mom.

He gained weight and was almost up to 160 lbs.

March 20, 2015

We had an appointment with Dad's oncologist today. The chemo has been working well. There are four rounds of chemo ordered but the next one will be altered a little bit to try to reduce the side effects. Dad has decided to continue with treatment.

Tonight he had a birthday party to attend. He joined in the celebration and spent some time with his siblings.

March 23, 2015

We were at the hospital early today for blood work and round two of chemo.

He felt good throughout the treatment and is having a good day.

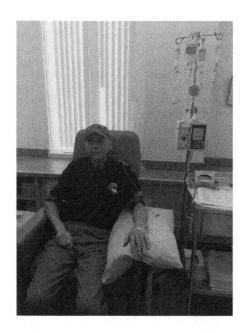

March 25, 2015

Dad had nausea and started vomiting today. He lost his appetite, is very tired and slept most of the day. He would get up long enough to have Ensure, Boost or water and go to the bathroom.

The trend continued until March 29th when he started getting his energy back and feeling good again.

We were able to have a great Easter celebration by keeping things simple. He was able to eat.

April 3, 2015

It is more bad news for Good Friday. We were told another family member was recently diagnosed with terminal cancer. Not news any of us were impressed to hear.

It was one foot in front of the other and one day at a time. If there was a lesson to be learned in all of this, it is enjoy the good minutes.

In the midst of the stress and worry that cancer can cause, you get to learn how strong love can be. It's powerful enough to make great memories in the worst situations, and is truly the only thing that provides the strength needed to make it through such an unbearable journey.

April 28, 2015

Dad had a rough night. When he took his pills at bedtime, he threw them up and continued to vomit all night. He suffered from nausea and was lethargic in the morning. Mom called and said she thought he would need to go to the hospital.

The palliative care nurse came to the house to check on Dad. She thought it would be good to go to the hospital too, but Dad wasn't in agreement. He wanted to stay at home. It is undetermined if how he is feeling is caused from the cancer, dehydration or the chemo.

I had been offered a Senior Account Manager position with Wireless City Inc., a Telus Platinum Business Excellence Dealer. I made the decision to accept the position after much discussion, thought and encouragement from the family. I went to the office and handed in my notice to terminate my position at the job I had been at for 15 years this morning.

Taya and Tiana took the day off of school to be with Dad.

Corie and I went over to Mom and Dad's house in the afternoon to convince Dad to go to the hospital. After a few hours of bargaining, he finally agreed, but was not happy about the situation.

He made it very clear that he was going on his terms and would leave on his terms. We were in agreement. We had arrangements made through the palliative care nurse so he was to be admitted right to 3B and connected to IV.

We had hoped to take him home after a few hours, but the blood work showed his potassium levels were high, he was very dehydrated and his kidneys were at risk of failing.

He demanded to be discharged three times and it took some desperate convincing to change his mind so he would stay. Frustrated and aggravated, he remained on IV and spent the night, but not without making it very clear on exactly what he thought of the whole situation. From here on out, it was going to be his way, and only his way.

Mom's brother was up and spent the afternoon with Dad at the hospital to keep him company. Something he had done many times while Dad was in the hospital.

April 29, 2015

Today, Dad was discharged from the hospital and had agreed that it was for the best that he came in overnight so that he could properly get rehydrated.

When Dad got out of the hospital this time, he was feeling better than he had in a long time. Home care was coming to the house for regular visits to help Mom and make sure things were going okay. Mom and Dad were able to go to do a few things and he was able to be at home.

One night they came over for supper and informed Corie and I that they were going to sell the house and move into a condo. Keeping up with the yard and the house was getting to be too much work and it was time to have something simple. The stairs were just too much and it would be for the best. He wanted it done as soon as possible, which was understandable.

They lived in their house for over forty years, and Dad was a very organized hoarder, keeping everything, just in case he would need it one day.

They had our support on the decision, but with everything going on, the timing was overwhelming. Everything happened very quickly. Mom made a few calls, contacted a real estate agent, found a condo located close by where Corie and I live and made an appointment to go see it in two days.

When Mom and Dad went to look at the condo, Dad made it just past the entry way and into the kitchen before saying they would take it. He was so excited to get a place in the location they wanted at a good price. The deal was done and possession was set for June 1, 2015.

We had an appointment with the oncologist. He strongly recommended that Dad not go through another round of chemo. When Dad asked him for an educated guess on how much time he had left, based on others in similar situations, the doctor responded that he had no idea of knowing for sure, but if he was forced to guess, possibly another few months. Dad opted to have another round of chemo.

His granddaughter, Taya, was graduating from high school on May 30th. He was hoping to be strong enough to make it to her prom.

He also wanted to clean out his garage, spend at least a day at the new condo and have time to enjoy the summer.

ACCEPTANCE

May 17, 2015

Today there were some visitors. Dad was excited to let people know that they were selling the house and tell them all about the new condo. Later in the afternoon, he was getting tired.

After everyone left, he and I were sitting on the deck talking. He looked at me with the most serious look, and said, "Dead has got to be better than this you know". He was sick of feeling sick all the time, and who could blame him. He fought so hard and did everything he could. His body was giving out, and he knew it.

Dad wanted the house to go up for sale right away. It took him some convincing that it would be better to wait until they were settled into their condo. This way they will not have to be concerned about leaving when he isn't feeling well for potential buyers to come look at the house once it is listed. He finally agreed.

May 18, 2015

It was another round of chemo today. Taya stayed with him and we were all popping in and out to visit with him. When it was done, we got him home, but it didn't take long for the nausea to kick in. The medication wasn't helping this time.

Mom stayed up with him all night at the side of the bed while he got sick. Defeat settled in and they cried as Dad realized his medical oncologist and Mom were right, taking this last round of chemo definitely a mistake. He told Mom that if it wasn't for her, he would have been dead a long time ago.

May 19, 2015

Home care came in to try to help him. He was getting dehydrated and it was recommended that he go to the hospital, but he didn't want to go. He was given additional medication for the nausea to see if it would help. Feeling terrible, he stayed in bed and Mom helped him the best she could.

May 20, 2015

He was feeling worse and home care came out again. We needed to get him rehydrated, but were respecting his wishes that only he would decide when he would go to the hospital. We were finally able to convince him he needed IV and the only way to get it was at the hospital. I promised to take him home the moment he wanted leave whether I thought it was a good idea or not. I wouldn't force him to stay at the hospital if he didn't want to. He finally agreed. Mom, Corie and I were able to get him into the vehicle. As he buckled his seat belt, he broke into tears and said, "This is the last time I will see this place". Hearts broken, we told him he would be back, took a moment before driving away and got him to the hospital.

When we arrived at emergency there wasn't a bed for him so we got stuck in the emergency room hallway across from the nursing station. They connected Dad to IV, but his vomiting was extreme. He was getting sick on average once every few minutes. Mom and I were rushing back and forth to the patient bathroom to empty the kidney shaped basin, wash it out and get it back to him before he got sick again.

Beside Dad in the hallway there was a homeless man that was constantly asking for a sandwich. He wreaked of stale alcohol, was wearing filthy clothing and had an entire loaf of bread sitting on his hospital bed with him. He was loud, obnoxious and Dad was forced to endure listening to him repeatedly yell at the nurse for a sandwich or a drink. This continued for hours while Dad was stuck in the hallway, gravely ill and constantly vomiting without any privacy.

Dad and I were able to convince Mom to go home and get some rest while I stayed with him in emergency. She had been up all night with him and was worn out.

The vomiting wasn't slowing down. Getting tired from running back and forth to the patient bathroom emptying the basin, frustration peaked when there were two hospital employees, sitting behind the nursing station, playing on their cell phones. I asked them if what they were doing on their phones was more important that helping to take care of my Dad. Their response was, "It is not our job. The nurse handles that." I responded, "It isn't my job either, can you find a nurse?" The two employees had the decency to stay out of my sight while playing on their cell phones after that.

The homeless man needed to go to the bathroom and a nurse came to help him. As he walked by Dad's bed, he started yelling, "I hate the smell of death. That man smells like death. That man is dying". The nurse was mortified and apologized, but Dad started to cry and continued to vomit.

We were moved to a private room shortly after that, but medication wasn't working. Corie came and the two of us were running back and forth between Dad and the bathroom for a while. Dad, frustrated, let the nurse on duty know that if it wasn't for his family, he was sure he would have been dead already. Eventually, they found a medication that worked and he was moved to 3A, the palliative ward, into a private room that was accommodating for family to stay with him. He finally got settled and got some sleep.

On that ward, there were old country music CD's that he enjoyed listening to, a TV, a couch that we could lay down on in his room, a hide-a-bed and the nurses were incredible.

He was grateful that the medication was working and was seeming to get a little better, but then took a turn for the worse. He was getting weaker. Getting an IV into his arm was virtually impossible. There were only two nurses in the hospital that we knew could get the needle into his very tricky rolling veins without too much pain. Eventually it wasn't working for them either and he just refused IV.

He didn't want to go home because he thought he would lose his room and be stuck in emergency again if he had to come back.

One day when Corie came to visit, he took Dad outside for a cigarette and Dad came up with a brainwave. He knew Mom was at home planting petunias. He wanted to go home to see her and hoped she would come back with them to the hospital.

Corie wheeled him across the parking lot toward his truck. They were almost at the vehicle when someone yelled, "Hey, where do you think you are going?" For a moment, Dad panicked because he thought he was caught by the hospital staff, but quickly realized it was just his nephew and wife coming to visit him. He let them know that he was breaking out to go home for a minute. They understood and let him make his get-a-way.

When he got home, he was so excited to see his long-time friends and neighbors for a good visit. He got to see the house, look at the flowers and go for a drive. He did all of that without losing his room and he was thrilled.

After the trip home, he started to deteriorate quickly. It was only a few days before the whole family was staying at the hospital with him full-time. We didn't leave him day or night.

His voice was getting weak and he was concerned what would happen when we couldn't hear him anymore. We let him know, that if necessary, he could squeeze our hand and we would always figure out a way to communicate. It eventually got to that point.

On 3A, there is a beautiful solarium that we found after Dad had already slipped into a state that he was sleeping most of the time. The nurses helped us wheel him into the room so he would have a different view if he woke up.

His eyes were cloudy when he opened them. He was very dehydrated. We couldn't give him water because he would choke, so we attempted to swab his mouth instead. Eventually, that little amount of water caused him to choke too.

It was warm in the solarium so Corie lifted him upright and was trying to swab his mouth and get him to spit out any excess water so he wouldn't choke. When he got him into a good position, Corie said, "Ok Dad, do it now". Out of nowhere, Dad completely frustrated, yelled, "DO WHAT?" We were all taken back. He was barely able to whisper for days, but that came out very loud and very clear. We couldn't help but laugh.

He laid back and turned his head towards the window. As he looked out the window he said, "it's close". I asked him if he wanted to be moved closer to the window. He shook his head frustrated and responded, "so stupid". We couldn't help but laugh again.

We had a good afternoon in there with him before taking him back to his room to get settled in.

May 27, 2016

Today, he started Cheyne Stokes. His breath was so laboured we were scared to leave him for a minute.

May 28th, 2016

His brothers, sister and a friend came to visit him today but he wasn't awake. Mom sat up by his side all night long, holding his hand, expecting that he wouldn't make the night.

At 8 am, we finally convinced her to get some sleep. She is completely worn out.

May 29th, 2016

The family is having to make a tough decision.

Tomorrow is Taya's prom. We don't want to leave him for a moment in the event that he wakes up and we aren't there, but we don't want to force Taya to go to her prom without us there to support her either. She is graduating as valedictorian, with five university credits and several scholarships.

We decided we will have family come and sit with him for a few hours if need be so that he isn't alone and we will all go to the prom together for a while and come back to the hospital after the supper. He is sleeping most of the time and waking up for maybe five minutes a day.

Today, I got his final tear on a handkerchief.

May 30, 2016

Mom and Corie spent the night in the room with Dad. At about 6 am he had briefly woke up and was calling for Mom, then went back to sleep. We had been timing how many breaths he was taking in a minute when the nurse came in to let us know that sometimes they just want to be alone.

That was never what he told us, but she did let us know that sometimes they change their minds.

The girls went home to get ready for the graduation and had plans to have a fun morning. Mom, Corie and I left him for about fifteen minutes to go to the cafeteria to grab something to eat. I'm not certain that any of us chewed our food before rushing back up to his hospital room. Corie decided to take time to go for a cigarette before coming back up.

Mom, Corie and I were sitting by his side at 11:11 am when he took his last breath and peacefully released it at 11:13 am. Allen came into the world surrounded by family that loved him and it is how he left. We stayed with him until his body was taken away.

With broken hearts filled with relief and grief, we gathered his things and left the hospital. Grateful that the suffering was done and overwhelmed with figuring out how to go on without him, we made our way home to make phone calls before going to the graduation.

Dad had been thinking of a good day to die for some time. When he was five, he lost his Dad and missed him every day of his life, thinking of him often. He believed May 30th was his father's birthday. He always said, when your number is up, it is up. Allen Triffo found a great number and made the most of his dash!

In the end, it got to the point that watching him suffer and deteriorate knowing that nothing could be done was worse than letting him go so that his pain would stop. There are no words to describe the suffering he endured or the pain it caused us to watch him have to go through it.

We are all familiar with what it feels like to have a shattered heart, but we have managed to carry on. It's what he would expect.

Dad was not a man to dwell on the past. He focused on what he could do and if there was nothing that could be done, he would forget about it, or at least try to.

Every day that Dad's eyes opened was a blessing. Every challenge that came with the day, we got through with the hope of having another good minute. Every minute is an adventure and we don't know for sure what each day holds for any of us. There are no guarantees. Life can change in an instant, for the better or worse.

If you've lost a loved one, you probably know the feeling of wishing you had a minute to spend with that person to ask a question, tell them a story, share a laugh or give them a hug. That is how I suggest spending time with your loved ones while you have the chance.

Allen Triffo is always in our thoughts and embedded in our hearts. We miss him dearly, every day. I expect that will never go away.

THE FINAL PREPARATIONS

Dad never had to make choices alone. Mom, Corie and I were at every doctor's appointment he had. We researched information, shared our perspectives and explained our reasoning for them. The ultimate decision was always Dad's but the agreements were made as a family. He was always fully supported in whatever he decided, even if it wasn't what we would have chosen for ourselves because he was the one stuck in his body. We let him do things his way, as much as possible.

There is peace that comes from knowing that everything within our means, and his comfort level, that could be done, was done.

On May 31, Mom, Corie and I sat down to make our first decision without him. We had to decide when the funeral would be held. We knew what he wanted, but had to decide on a date.

Corie had been in the process of purchasing Printwest, the largest printing shop in Saskatchewan, for the past several months. Being with Dad at the hospital had taken priority over everything else and he had missed a lot of work. It needed to be his priority to catch up. With nothing else that could be done to help Dad, it was his preference not to do the service during a weekday.

Mom was taking possession of the condo that she and Dad had purchased on June 1, 2015. There was a lot of work required deciding what was going to be taken to the condo, sorting through everything and getting the house ready to be sold. It wasn't an immediate rush, but she wanted to get it taken care of sooner than later.

There were a lot of things that had to be done with the estate, forms that needed to be filled out and decisions in preparing the final farewell.

Taya was valedictorian and her graduation ceremonies were coming up at the end of June. We needed to be sure that there was enough time between the funeral and the graduation to give her a degree of separation. She had already had to go to prom on the day her grandpa passed away and we were sensitive to that.

Tiana wanted to say a poem. Her grandpa was one of her favorite people and they had been virtually inseparable from the time she was born. There had to be enough time for her to process everything and prepare so she could get through it without putting added pressure on herself.

I was being certified as a Life and Executive Coach on the upcoming weekend. The following weekend, I was scheduled to be in Winnipeg for a National Board Meeting and had a course booked with an instructor from Barcelona, Spain. I was also scheduled to fly to Edmonton to meet with my new employer. My new position was scheduled to start July 2nd.

Taking all of these factors into consideration, the next possible date that would for everyone was June 20. That would have been Dad's 67th birthday with the following day being Father's Day. It was the beginning of our "year of firsts". We decided having his funeral that day would be the perfect way to celebrate the life of an amazing man, husband, father, grandfather, son, brother, uncle, nephew, cousin, brother-in-law, friend, co-worker and neighbour.

On June 20, 2015 a celebration of Allen Triffo's life was shared with those that loved him. Some of his favorite country songs were played, his favorite flowers (tiger lilies) were at the front of the church and a beautiful booklet was prepared for the attendees with pictures that were a great representation of his life.

His grandchildren read a poem, I read a eulogy, but it was the heartfelt and honest stories about Allen, shared by Corie that moved everyone in attendance. They were entertaining and a true representation of who he really was. The minister gave his sermon and birthday cake was served at the luncheon following the service.

Allen Triffo was laid to rest in the family plot at the Bulyea Cemetery. It is a beautiful spot located on a hill under a tree, just like he requested. Close family and friends were in attendance. Immediately after his burial, an orange butterfly, the same colour as the tiger lilies, flew over his grave. It was a beautiful end for a cherished life.

July 2015, Sandra was able to move into her condo and eventually sold the house.

Taya graduated and did a wonderful job presenting her valedictory speech. She started university in the fall.

Tiana got her licence and made honor roll for her Grade 11 year.

Corie completed the purchase of Printwest. It took a while, but he eventually went back to spending time restoring vehicles and racing his car.

I am now a published author. My passion continues to be to help people get back on track when "life happens" so that they can spend time doing what they love.

This book is dedicated in memory of my Dad, Allen Triffo. He was the rock in our family. He spoke up for what he believed in, had no fear in letting others know what he thought and had little tolerance for things that didn't make sense.

When diagnosed with cancer, he faced each day with courage and unshakeable strength. He wanted to see improvements in the health care system.

If this helps one patient and his/her family, the effort will be worth it. To someone, that patient, may be the center of his/her world and the one person they can't imagine living without.

Our family knows what it feels like to lose that one person.

Dad, this one is for you.

Love Always,

Your Family

xoxo

Fear Trumps Logic

If ever faced with a serious illness, having a doctor diagnose me based on suspicion, would not ease my mind. Confirmed facts, based on evidence from my body is what I expect.

The outcome of Dad's illness would have likely lead to the same result. He believed when your number is up, there is nothing that can be done. However, the journey to the destination definitely could have been better. One accurate diagnosis in September or early October, edible food in the hospital and an improved admissions process would have made the emotional journey more comfortable for him.

When my vehicle is taken for auto repair, the mechanic doesn't look at it for a few minutes, listen to it run and start guessing what to repair. I definitely do not pay to have fluids changed, then drive it for ten days, just to see if that fixes the problem. My vehicle is hooked up to diagnostic equipment that has codes from the manufacturer designed to detect what the issue is. Once that is complete, the mechanic informs me of what repairs are required and I give approval for it to be fixed. There are times that further investigation is required, but the process always makes logical sense.

There are individuals that are comfortable with a doctor looking at them for a few minutes, checking their vitals and then they are happy to get a prescription to take for ten days, based on an educated guess, without testing, to see if it helps make them feel better. If that doesn't work, they go back to their doctor to try another prescription while potentially waiting for tests. Bodies are more complex and precious than vehicles. This trial and error mentality confuses me. Vehicles are easy to replace, but humans only get one body to live in for a lifetime.

The prescription medication commercials baffle me. They spend a few seconds talking about the benefits of the prescription and the majority of the time warning about potential side effects. For some, the last precaution is, "and may cause death". There are people that take these medications because the benefits are supposed to outweigh the risks. What benefit outweighs the possible cause of death? If the medication causes death, the best case scenario would be someone saying sorry to your family as they prepare your funeral arrangements. Call me crazy, but if I am prescribed a medication that lists "may cause death" on the sheet with the long list of side effects, I am happy to look for another solution to feel better.

The first time you hear a doctor say the words, "we have found a mass and are checking for cancer", speaking from a loved one's perspective, it is traumatic. I can't imagine what it would be like to be caged in the body of the person to whom those words are directed. Worry will not fix anything, but the mind struggles desperately between hoping for the best and fearing the worst. It is a situation that too many are faced with and no one deserves.

The worst news you can get is there is nothing that can be done and the only measures that can be taken are designed to delay the inevitable. In this case, affairs are put in order and the priority becomes seizing good moments while the opportunity is available. It is a great way for everyone to live.

Facts based on the patients reality is important for the emotional and physical well-being of everyone involved in these trying situations, including the doctors.

Doctors are human. They have Ph. D's and experience, but they do not hold the blueprint for every human being. With patients holding onto every word they say as gospel, it puts physicians in a difficult situation where they are forced to guess at what symptoms could be if the resources for a confirmed diagnosis are not readily available. In this situation, the patient still holds that physician accountable and expects them to be correct based on an educated guess.

This environment puts doctors and the health care system at risk of losing credibility. It is not their fault. Their hearts are in the right place, everyone is doing what they can, but resources are limited.

This book was written to raise awareness to start efforts to get necessary diagnostic tools to reduce wait times and increase accurate diagnosis for patients by providing doctors with the test results required to do their jobs efficiently and effectively.

My hope is that the citizens of southern Saskatchewan, if ever faced with hearing those challenging words, will have the opportunity to get an accurate diagnosis, as quickly as possible, so they have the chance to choose the best treatment plan for them.

May these people live their good minutes knowing that everything that can be done is being done.

THE MISSION

Allen Triffo never gave up.

Against all odds, when everyone was convinced he wouldn't make it out of the hospital after collapsing, he found the strength to get well enough to go home for almost three months. The word "quit" was not in his vocabulary. At the end, he pushed his body as far as it would allow and then he survived for another four days. Eventually, he gave himself the permission to let go. His will, drive and determination was the exception rather than the norm.

The vision and mission were created with his survivor mentality in mind. It includes what he knew would have made his struggles in the last few months a better experience. The intent is to help implement positive change for future patients. It is understood that there are challenges and obstacles.

"If you always do what you've always done, you'll always get what you always gotten". ~Tony Robbins

Mission Statement: Work with Hospitals of Regina Foundation and the people of southern Saskatchewan to raise funds for diagnostics to be improved in the region.

Vision Statement: Saskatchewan citizens have access to the diagnostic tools required to have a confirmed diagnosis within days in a facility that promotes a positive, healthy and healing environment.

These journals are intended to help the public understand what it can be like dealing with a terminal illness for patients and their loved ones.

The choices we made as a family may be different than what you would choose. We are all individuals with different training, ideas, beliefs, resources and comfort levels.

This book is not intended to encourage anyone to make the same decisions or imply that someone else diagnosed with lung cancer would have the same experience as Allen. It is simply a true story about his journey that explains how perspectives change, outlines the grieving process experienced with this cancer diagnosis (it will be different for everyone), and share the struggles faced in the healthcare system to express how important it is to have a proper diagnosis as soon as possible.

Getting mad and pointing blame will not fix anything. It won't bring him, and others that have had similar experiences, back to life. Being a part of the solution rather than complaining about the problem is the best way to implement improvements.

Doctors, nurses and pharmacists understand medicine and how the body reacts to them. These are the experts needed when things go seriously wrong. If I am in a car accident, I want the best doctor and surgeon that can be found to help put me back together.

If an individual does not want to make lifestyle changes, or a disease is too advanced, numbing the symptom maybe the only way for the individual to experience relief.

Hippocrates said, "Let food be your medicine". A naturopath is an expert on how food can help the body heal itself. I believe hospitals working with these experts, to help patients get the nutrients they need to regain health, would reduce pressure on the health care system. Their knowledge is valuable and would be beneficial to utilize.

Today, there will be someone in a hospital waiting to get their test results, someone in the community waiting to get a test taken while knowing there is something really wrong and someone taking their last breath wishing there was something that could have been done.

Until there is a cure, we need to work together to improve the health care system to make these difficult times better for the patients, their families and the people that spend their days working with them.

When waiting for a diagnosis, the ideas and theories can be as vast as the perspectives on circle rainbows. We all have one body to last a lifetime. When trying to regain health, I choose fact over theory.

~ THE END ~

Journals of a Loved One Photo Gallery:
www.calyndatriffo.com

HOW TO BE PART OF THE SOLUTION

TAX DEDUCTIBLE DONATIONS

Hospitals of Regina Foundation has set up a "diagnostic fund". This fund will be used for diagnostic improvements within the region.

TO DONATE:

- ❖ Go To Website: www.hrf.sk.ca
- ❖ Click on the donate icon
- ❖ Fill in donation information form
- ❖ Choose designation: "Diagnostic Fund"
- ❖ Complete by pressing "Donate Now"

A sincere thank you to all that make a contribution to help improve the health care system. Every little bit matters and it is appreciated!

FUNDRAISING CAMPAIGNS

Fundraising Updates: www.calyndatriffo.com

To add a fundraiser to the website, please send an email to: calyndatriffo@sasktel.net

SHARE YOUR IDEAS WITH ME ON SOCIAL MEDIA:

Links available at: www.calyndatriffo.com

COMING SOON

JOURNALS OF THE SURVIVORS

Everyone is born unique. When critical illness is diagnosed, there is an emotional journey involved. Reactions to the news varies for everyone. Fear is a factor, their own fears and those of their loved ones.

There is a common denominator among survivors. They have confidence, peace and determination in regaining their health. They hear the diagnosis, but do not really accept the outcome of the norm. A driving force is something they are determined to live for and they decide the only option is for things to go their way. Illness is considered a temporary inconvenience.

All of them did what they needed to for the illness to be treated. They didn't run from their symptoms, they faced the challenge head on and researched treatments.

Once the symptoms were under control, they kept an open mind and have implemented lifestyle changes for prevention and optimum health. Perspective and priorities have shift and the lessons they learned on the journey have improved their lives. Their focus was, and still is, on living and enjoying every moment to the fullest.

In this book, I will introduce you to the survivors that continue to win every day and others that are completely symptom free. It is an honor to be in the presence of their amazing outlook on life.

There have been survivors that beat critical illness using western medicine while others used alternative health care modalities or a combination of both. Some have been diagnosed with months to live and they survived years. Others were given a very low chance of survival based on statistics and beat the odds. Experience has taught me that everyone has their own journey.

There have been countless posts on social media, articles and debates where individuals are determined to prove what they believe is right and the only way of doing things. People gravitate to what they have been taught and most follow blind faith, never really investigating anything different before fighting to prove their point.

Many follow the advice or adopt belief systems from parents, grandparents and teachers who follow the same information that was taught to them. What if those people just didn't know another way? I recommend investigating all possibilities and then use the one that works best for you based on results, not theory. It's that simple.

Understanding how your body reacts to different things, what makes you feel better and knowing when something just isn't right is important in the healing process. You are the one that is living in your body.

As a loved one, the best way to support anyone is to respect their choices and decisions. Whatever provides peace is the best option.

I once asked a terminal patient, "If you were on the Titanic when it hit the iceberg and was starting to sink, what would you do?" The response was, "Go down with the ship", I was shocked. Today, that would be the furthest thing from my mind. I would be busy finding a life jacket and a scuba suit to prepare for the swim if there wasn't room in a life boat.

Note: I can't swim.

Accepting that we all have an expiry date, it is understandable that someone would make that choice once they come to terms with the fact that their bodies are not able to provide them with the quality of life that they want. In my opinion, a survivor is someone that makes the choice to focus on living as long as their eyes open and they are able to breathe.

The survivors I know, when told that something is impossible, find a way to move the apostrophe so it becomes I'm possible. Their bodies have the strength they need to get through the day and they have the will to survive. They still experience fear, struggles, pain, depression and all the other emotions associated with it, but they hold onto their purpose for living and fight for their good minutes facing each challenge as it comes, one moment at a time. They find a way for logic to trump fear.

If 99% of the population believes that there isn't a solution, a survivor hunts to find the 1% thing that will make a difference and try it. They always ask questions and do not stop until they have an answer that works. They trust their survival instincts over everything else.

Their questions start with how and what. Love is usually the driving force behind their desires and they have a purpose. That determination is a gift.

I am happy to introduce you to some of these individuals. With the odds stacked against them, they overcame challenges that most would never want to face.

These are the journals of the survivors.

62395791R00092

Made in the USA
Charleston, SC
15 October 2016